LOVE AND LONGBOARD

ONE MAN'S FAITH JOURNEY ACROSS AMERICA, 3,200 MILES ON A SKATEBOARD, AND NOTHING BUT LOVE FOR EVERYONE ALONG THE WAY

DANIEL HERMAN JR.

WINDPATH PRESS

An Imprint of the Herman Leadership Foundation

Published in Greenville, South Carolina by Windpath Press, an imprint of the Herman Leadership Foundation.

This book may be purchased in bulk for educational, business, fundraising, or sales promotional use. For information, please e-mail hello@loveandlongboard.com

Substantive Edit by Geoffrey Stone, ClearWords Group
Copy Edit by Brooks Becker
Proofread by Blair Parke
Cover design by Marko Markovic, 5MediaDesign
Typeset by Dawn Black
Cover imagery provided courtesy of Loaded Boards

ISBN 979-8-9994750-0-8 (Paperback)
ISBN 979-8-9994750-1-5 (Hardback)
ISBN 979-8-9994750-2-2 (eBook – EPUB)
ISBN 979-8-9994750-3-9 (eBook – Kindle)
ISBN 979-8-9994750-4-6 (Audiobook – Digital)

Library of Congress Control Number: 2025920194

Printed in the United States of America

Interested in ordering 10 or more copies for your group, school or organization? Email hello@loveandlongboard.com for special bulk pricing.

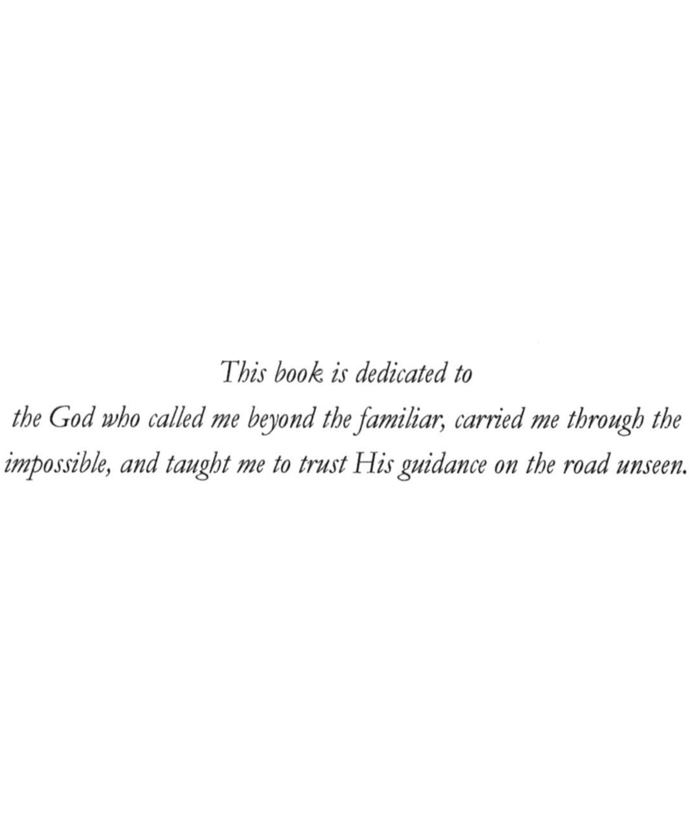

This book is dedicated to

the God who called me beyond the familiar, carried me through the impossible, and taught me to trust His *guidance on the road unseen.*

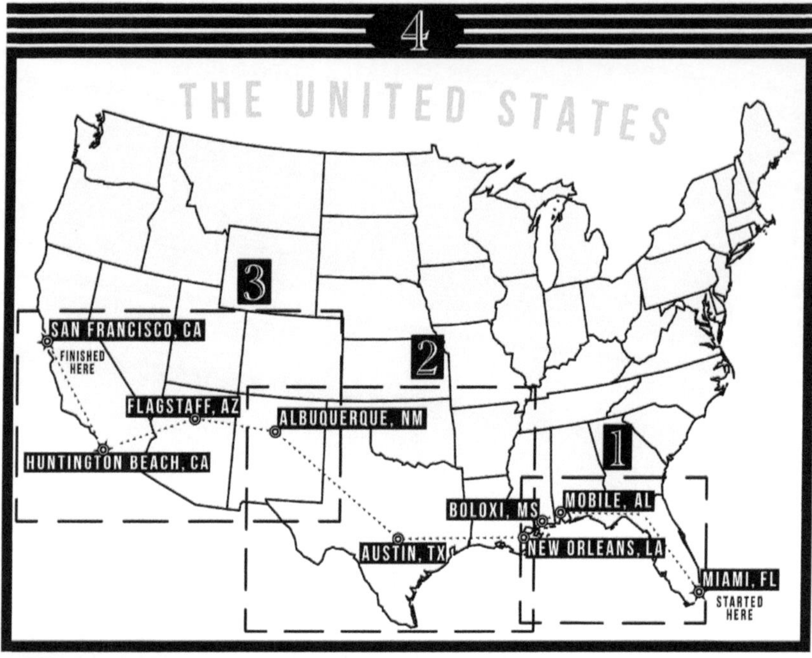
4
THE UNITED STATES
3
2
1
SAN FRANCISCO, CA
FINISHED HERE
FLAGSTAFF, AZ
ALBUQUERQUE, NM
HUNTINGTON BEACH, CA
BOLOXI, MS
MOBILE, AL
AUSTIN, TX
NEW ORLEANS, LA
MIAMI, FL
STARTED HERE

San Francisco
San Jose
Santa Cruz
Monterey
NEVADA
UTAH
COLORADO
CALIFORNIA
Santa Barbara
Thousand Oaks
Culver City
Huntington Beach
Bullhead City
Twentynine Palms
Vidal
Flagstaff
Holbrook
Gallup
Albuquerque
Moriarty
SantaRosa
Texico
66
PACIFIC OCEAN
ARIZONA
NEW MEXICO
TEXAS
3

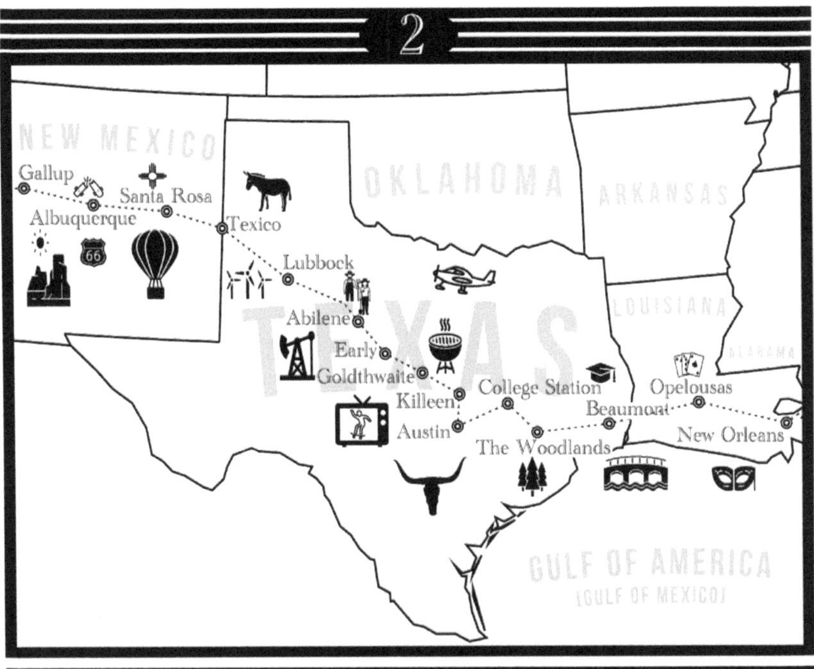

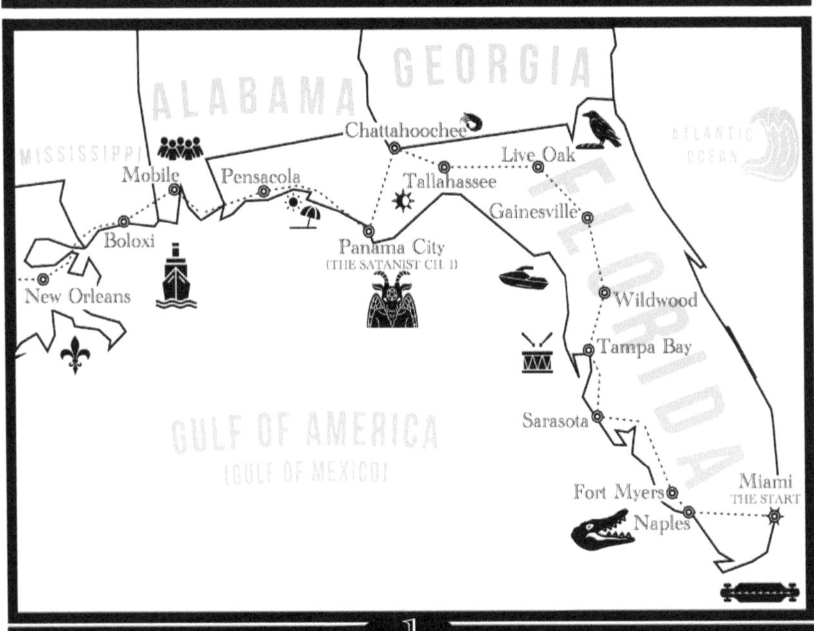

ARTWORK © DESIGNED BY DANIEL HERMAN JR.

CONTENTS

INTRODUCTION

"Did you really longboard across America?"

Yes, I longboarded (a type of skateboard) across the United States from the East Coast to the West Coast. Whenever I say this to someone, it almost always sparks some curiosity that is typically paired with a question. Many people ask me one or two questions, but then there are those relentless individuals who never cease with their questions. I love it though; it provides the opportunity to share the most unbelievable stories, from sleeping at the house of a satanist to receiving bread from a raven. Another time, I was nearly arrested by the cops for attending a church service and toward the end of my journey, I had my longboard stolen at a Starbucks in California after using it to cross more than 3,000 miles of the country. Each incident adds a unique chapter to my journey. I don't mind all the questions; I love telling stories. If you picked up this book, you probably like reading stories. And you're probably wondering why I was sleeping at a satanist's house in the first place, right?

Like anything else in life, it takes some practice to tell a good story. I think we all can tell a good story when we're passionate about it. There was a time when I doubted my storytelling abilities, but when you get your longboard stolen from you after riding it across the country, everyone wants to know if you got it back, and that's exactly how my storytelling skills began to grow. Some of my tales are well-worn from repetition, yet others linger in the shadows, awaiting the right moment for a proper telling to others. This book is my attempt to give the best of those stories the proper time and space they truly deserve to be appreciated.

People told me years before I ever set out that if I finished my skateboard journey, I should write a book to capture the lessons I would learn and the adventures I would experience along the way. With that in mind, I made sure to journal every day, noting where I was, the miles and routes I traveled, the names of significant places and people I saw and met, and the unique moments that unfolded along the way. Most of the names and details in this book are true, though a few have been changed to protect the privacy of those individuals.

Traveling across the United States as a young adult made me realize how much my worldview was shaped by my Christian upbringing. I feel as though I didn't really choose my beliefs as a child because I never questioned them; they were more like ideas I inherited, shaped by how I grew up. However, through my longboard journey, I began to see things differently. Along the way, people questioned and criticized my beliefs, which pushed me to examine them more closely and make sure they were true. I gained new insights through conversations, encounters, circumstances, and mainly by reading the Bible cover to cover for the first time. Each of these moments challenged what I thought I understood and reshaped the way I saw the truth.

Each chapter that follows tells a real story from my journey, contrasting what I once thought to be true with the beliefs I hold today. With every push westward, what I once imagined about the world gave way to new beliefs; I've recorded them at the beginning of each chapter. I know my mind is not perfect, and with time, I may see things differently, but this is the place I stand today. I am convinced my understanding will continue to improve as the Holy Spirit leads me into deeper truth through the adventures still ahead.

As a father myself, I know how important it is to guide what our kids read and consume. This book tells real stories from my journey, including conversations with people who hold a variety of perspectives, worldviews, philosophies, religions, and even sexual preferences. In each encounter, I share my Christian faith, but the dialogue may contain things you'd prefer your child not hear just yet. For that reason, I'd encourage you to read the book first and decide when the timing feels right for your family.

Now, before diving into the chapters of this book, I want to pause and answer some of the most common questions people ask when they hear that I longboarded across the United States.

Top 10 Typical Questions

1. "How long did that take you?"

This is the number one question so many people instinctively ask me. And many are surprised to hear that it took me nearly two years to finish. That's because after longboarding for the first six months, I took an unexpected break for a full year. Then I returned to where I had left off and finished the trip in the final six months.

2. "Where and when did you start and finish your trip?"

My original goal was to travel coast to coast on my longboard from Virginia Beach, Virginia, to Los Angeles, California, but then I decided to begin in the southwest corner of Miami, Florida, longboard to Los Angeles, and then travel up to San Francisco, California. So, I started my journey at South Point Pier in Miami Beach, Florida on Thursday, January 18, 2018. I met a random guy named Johnny on the pier that day. His close friend had just passed away, so he rode to South Point on his longboard hoping to find some peace. When we saw each other riding longboards, we began a nice conversation at the end of the pier while looking out over the Atlantic Ocean. Toward the end of our interaction, I told Johnny that I was about to longboard across America. He looked at me with the biggest eyes of surprise and said, "Are you serious right now?" I definitely was. When it came time to start, Johnny longboarded down the pier with me toward the land, and when we reached the concrete sidewalk, I said, "San Francisco, here I come! See ya later, Johnny!" and flashed him the Shaka sign. I was on my way to the Golden Gate Bridge.

Almost two years later, I completed my coast-to-coast goal and jumped in the Pacific Ocean, just south of L.A., in Huntington Beach, California, on Sunday, October 27, 2019. It was a very special moment for me, and it was also the day after my twenty-fifth birthday. Even though I had made it coast to coast, I didn't stop there but continued "traveling" north. I say traveling because I didn't longboard the whole way up California's coast. After two more months of traveling and some longboarding, I finally arrived in San Francisco and longboarded across the Golden Gate Bridge, where I officially ended my trip on December 7, 2019.

3. "How many miles was that?"

I longboarded approximately 3,200 miles (5,150 kilometers), though the total distance I traveled was closer to 3,800 miles (6,100 kilometers). For the miles when I wasn't on the board, I was either walking or, on rare occasions, riding in a vehicle. Once, after completing my coast-to-coast goal, I flew over a 200-mile stretch of California to avoid the treacherous terrain of Big Sur.

For context, the shortest coast-to-coast bicycle route on Google Maps is about 2,700 miles (4,200 kilometers). My original plan was to cover every mile by pushing or walking with the board and never accept a ride. But after my first 1,000 miles of solo longboarding, a police officer forced me to get in his vehicle, and the streak was broken. From then on, I stayed on the board the majority of the time or walked when roads were too rough. If someone offered me a ride, I almost always said no. On the rare occasions I accepted, it was either when safety was at stake or when I felt it was a connection I was meant to make. I never once asked for a ride until after I had already completed the coast-to-coast goal, when I needed help crossing a mountain in California between Santa Cruz and San Jose.

Starting way down in southern Florida added nearly 500 extra miles before I even began heading west, which made my total journey longer than the distance across the country itself. In the end, I was physically on the longboard for about 3,200 miles. Since the coast-to-coast distance is only 2,700 miles, I can confidently say that I longboarded across America, and it's way easier than explaining everything. I wasn't chasing a record. I was chasing a journey, and the journey was enough for me.

4. "How many sets of wheels/boards/shoes did you go through?"

I went through four sets of wheels—all different colors, one board, and too many shoes! Ok, maybe it was like five pairs of shoes, but I couldn't tell you because I didn't keep track. And, to answer the most common follow-up question: No, I didn't keep a set of spare wheels with me in my backpack. In fact, I was continually surprised with how each set of wheels were provided for me along the way.

5. "Would you longboard on the highways and interstates?"

I would longboard anywhere as long as it was west, but I preferred paved roads, bike routes, sidewalks, and the shoulders of main roads. I would also longboard on the shoulders of US state highways, which is perfectly legal, but the US Interstate System has different rules. I did my best to avoid them, but there came a time when the interstate was the only good option. I saw signs that said NO PEDESTRIANS ALLOWED, *but I didn't consider myself a pedestrian and began longboarding down I-40 starting in Santa Rosa, New Mexico. Seventy miles (113 kilometers) down the road, I was pulled over by a state trooper, but, after I told him that I was "longboarding across America," he thought that was cool and let me go. The same thing happened in Arizona, but this time the cop said, "Pedestrians aren't allowed on this interstate, only bicycles." I tried to argue that I wasn't a pedestrian, but he responded with, "Because your feet touch the ground as you ride, you're considered a pedestrian." Then he gave me a written warning but was nice enough to let me keep going.*

6. "How old were you when you first started longboarding?"

Well, I stepped on a skateboard for the first time when I was eight years old and fell in love! Skateboarding and longboarding are essentially the same thing. The difference is that skateboards tend to be shorter, longboards are longer, hence the name, and longboards typically have bigger wheels. When I was eight, I didn't even know what a longboard was, but when I was a teenager, my older sister, Audrey, came home from college with something she called a longboard. I was impressed! That summer, I saved enough money to buy my first longboard. I wanted one that was good quality and looked nice. I went to a skate shop nearby and found a bunch of different longboards there. After standing on all of them and riding around the store, I bought the most expensive one: the Tan Tien (Flex 3) made by Loaded Boards. I liked it because it was made of bamboo and fiberglass, creating the most comfortable ride. I was seventeen years old when I first started longboarding and fell in love all over again.

7. "So, what board did you use on your trip across America?"

I thought my Tan Tien Loaded board was great, but I hadn't ridden much of anything else, so I wanted to investigate and see if I could find a better board. I had recently joined my sister at Northland International University in Dunbar, Wisconsin. It was there that I became known as the Longboard Guy because I would ride my Tan Tien board everywhere and would ask people to sign the bottom of it with a Sharpie. This made a lot of students want their own longboard, so I started buying different ones online, riding them for a bit, and then selling them to people on campus. I was able to test a plethora of boards to know precisely which ones I liked and didn't like. After a lot of testing, I found that Landyachtz was my second favorite, but my number one favorite was *still the Loaded Longboards; I just love their flexibility and versatility. Therefore, I stuck with the same brand but upgraded from the Tan Tien to the Loaded Dervish Sama—2015 edition (Flex 1) with the light blue Orangatang Wheels. <u>The longboard on the front cover of this book is the exact one I used on my trip across America, with all the people's signatures I collected along the way.</u>*

8. "Did you go alone?"

Yes, I went alone. Although I did have a lot of people tell me that they were interested in going with me, and another handful of people who confidently said, "I'll come with you," nobody ever did. I like to tell people that it was just me, my board, and the good Lord.

9. "Were you the first one to skateboard across America?"

No, there have been other guys who have done it, especially since 2018. And, as time goes on, even more people are attempting it.

10. "Where was the strangest place you ever stayed?"

Well, that would be at the home of a Couchsurfing host in Panama City, Florida. It was about six weeks into the trip when I unknowingly stepped into the house of a satanist. I was there to spend two nights. If you have more time, I would love to tell you my first story. It's the one that reveals the meaning of the famous words, "Love and Longboard."

↩

CHAPTER I.

THE SATANIST

FEBRUARY 27 – MARCH 1, 2018
CHATTAHOOCHEE TO PANAMA CITY, FLORIDA

I used to imagine that God only answered the prayers of the faithful churchgoer, but now I believe that He can answer the prayers of a satanist too.

The relentless Florida sun beat down on my shoulders, and with my mouth parched and water nearly gone, I walked with my longboard in hand, wondering if I would ever find my way back to a paved road. My backpack, heavy with all my belongings, especially my leather Bible, pressed against me. The gravel road stretched endlessly through the countryside and grain fields of Northern Florida. It was February 27, 2018, 6 weeks since I'd started my longboard journey across the United States, and I was officially lost for the first time.

The heat, though softened by the winter season, seemed to magnify my thirst with every step. Longboarding on the gravel road was too difficult, so I carried my board under my arm and trudged forward, hoping the road would change to pavement soon. A glance at my phone revealed no service, which meant no updates from Google Maps, only more gravel at the next crossroads. Frustrated but determined, I whispered, "God, please help me find a smooth road, so I can ride again."

Earlier that morning, I had set out from a Couchsurfing host's home just south of the Florida-Georgia line in the town of Chattahoochee. I stayed there for a couple of nights, resting after several weeks on the road. His name was Gene, and he was kind and generous. He cooked me gumbo, gave me a comfortable couch to sleep on, and introduced me to the two girlfriends he was dating. As we talked, he opened up about his life, sharing that he had once taken a cross-country trip with his son shortly before his son passed away at a young age. Encounters like this reminded me how God placed such unique people in my path, and I always tried to love them as I imagined Jesus would and share the gospel whenever an opportunity presented itself.

For those who don't know, Couchsurfing is an app that connects travelers with people willing to host them for free; it's against the community guidelines to charge for hosting. Couchsurfing is a mix between a social network and a hospitality exchange, where people open their homes to strangers, not for money but for the experience. Some hosts offer a spare bedroom, others just a couch or a spot on the floor. But it's more than a free place to crash. The real value is in the connections—sharing meals, swapping stories, and seeing a place through a local's eyes. For budget travelers or anyone seeking a deeper experience than just booking a hotel, it's a game-changer.

Leaving Gene's house that morning, I cruised west over the Chattahoochee Bridge on Highway 90, my wheels spinning swiftly over the concrete pavement. The sky greeted me with a stunning sunrise, splashing pinks, blues, and crisp whites across the horizon. I couldn't resist yelling, "GOOD MORNING, WORLD!" at the top of my lungs. It was fleeting moments like this that wove a sense of magic and awe into the fabric of my longboard journey.

On the other side of the river, the landscape began to shift. Sprawling fields, farmland, and thick woods replaced the small-town scenery. As the morning progressed, I called my Grandpa Herman; his voice always made the miles feel like minutes. Then the call dropped, as phone calls do when you are in the middle of nowhere. When I checked my map, I realized I had missed a turn somewhere back down the road. There was a choice to make: I could retrace my route and admit defeat, or I could hope that the gravel track in front of me would eventually lead back to pavement. I chose the gravel. Two hours later, the gravel and I had become well acquainted.

Then the first vehicle I had seen in hours roared by, a red pickup truck, kicking up a cloud of dust in my face. I was hoping they'd stop to help or at least offer water, but they didn't. I kept walking, growing more exhausted with each step. It was nearly impossible to longboard on this rough surface; the best comparison I can think of is like ice skating on a field of marbles. I prayed once more I'd find my way back to a paved road. After another half-hour of walking, I finally reached smooth pavement.

With a sigh of relief, I dropped my board to the ground and jumped on. The wheels spun effortlessly, the cool breeze hit my face again, and I felt a surge of hope. Confident now, I took my last sip of water and cruised down the highway, my speed increasing with every push.

Entering the outskirts of Panama City, it wasn't long before I spotted a small gas station off Highway 231. I left my board leaning near the entrance of the gas station, something I did often as I never locked it up or worried about it much. I figured if God could watch over me, He could watch over my board too. I hurried in the store to buy bottled water and lift it to my mouth. The moment the cold liquid touched my lips, I felt relief wash over me and was finally satisfied. With my thirst quenched, all that remained was to reach my next Couchsurfing host before nightfall.

He was expecting me since I had sent a request that he had accepted a few days earlier to stay at his apartment for two nights. His name was Martin, and he had many good reviews on his Couchsurfing profile. He was expecting me around 4 p.m., but I found myself running late because I had gotten lost. I was tired and hungry, but I couldn't stop yet. As I got closer to Martin's location, I called to give him an update. He sounded nice and offered to provide pizza for me once I got there, mentioning that a friend was helping him move a new sofa into his living room. "Pizza sounds amazing right now!" I exclaimed over the phone. Just the thought of a hot slice motivated me to quicken my pace.

Around six in the evening, I rolled into the heart of Panama City. The sun had slipped below the horizon, leaving the sky a kind of purplish black that felt like someone had dimmed the world. A row of townhouses ran along the left side of the road, their back porches facing the street. Martin's place was A3, so I squinted through the dark, looking for the right unit when a voice called out to me, "Is that you, Daniel?" There he was on the porch, mid-sofa maneuver, with a friend wrestling on the other side of the couch. They had the middle of the sofa balanced on the porch railing and were attempting to coax it through the sliding doors into the living room.

"Yeah, it's me!" I responded. "You must be Martin. Here, let me help you guys with that."

I hopped over the porch railing and grabbed the far side of the sofa while Chance, a neighbor about my age, held the other end. Martin stood on the porch, directing traffic like a conductor, his pleasant smile and round brown glasses gave him a professorial look. He was tall and lean, gray hair and a pointed nose that somehow suited the role. We set the sofa down and began putting it together with the other pieces. Martin had mentioned to me in our messages that he didn't have a bed for me to sleep on, only a new couch that would arrive the day I did.

"You didn't expect you'd have to build your own couch before sleeping on it. Did you, Dan? It's OK if I call you Dan, right?" Martin asked.

"Yeah Dan's fine, and no, I wasn't expecting to build anything tonight," I said with a laugh.

Martin had a dry wit and a calm poise. He tossed off one-liners, laughed at his own jokes, and said exactly what he thought without malice. Charming and refreshingly unfiltered, he could turn an awkward moment into something breezy, teasing you in a way that left you grinning. When Chance and I snapped the last pieces of the couch into place, I took a moment to look around. The living room was full of conversation-starting artwork: odd little sculptures, framed paintings on every wall, mirrors trimmed with golden trinkets, and a curious metal-and-plaster contraption on the far side that looked like someone had tried to build a robot from scrap and then given up halfway through. It was the kind of eclectic collection that makes a house feel lived in and interesting, the perfect backdrop for a new orange couch.

"If you couldn't already tell, I'm an artist," Martin proclaimed. "I painted most of these myself." He began showing off the paintings he was particularly proud of; many of them featured nude men striking various poses. Then he took me to the entryway where his most cherished artwork hung from the wall—a portrait of a man curled into the fetal position, arms wrapped tightly around his knees, gaze cast sideways. Bold strokes and textured layers brought out both the vulnerability of the man and the emotional weight behind his eyes.

"I'm also gay," Martin stated. "I don't like women very much, and Buddy doesn't either," referring to his little black-and-white terrier dog. "Since you're not a woman, Buddy will be your friend once he gets used to you, just like he did with Ethan—our newest housemate."

I bent down to let Buddy sniff my hand. He gave me a cautious glance, then backed away toward Martin's feet. Just then the front door squeaked as it opened. "Well, speak of the devil. Ethan, come in, come in. I want you to meet our latest wayfaring soul," Martin said, gesturing toward me with a half-empty wine glass. "Dan, this is Ethan. He's Navy. Just arrived for some top-secret training. Don't ask; we're not allowed to know."

Ethan looked back at Martin with a smirk and said, "If I told you, I'd have to kill you."

"Hah!" Martin laughed out loud. "Well, if you're going to do it, at least let me finish my wine first. You know I am very curious about your work. Anyway, Ethan moved in about a week ago, and I think we're gonna let him stay, but we're still deciding."

The three of us moved out of the entryway into the kitchen when Chance called out from the living room, "Alright, Martin, now that the couch is finally installed, it's your turn to buy the pizza."

Martin grinned from the kitchen and called back, "Of course, I'll buy the pizza, but I'm picking the toppings, and don't even think about complaining. Now, Dan, would you like a glass of wine?"

"I'm good, Martin. I don't drink but thank you."

Then Ethan placed a fresh plate of shrimp up on the counter that he had picked up from the store. He made a cocktail sauce from scratch that was delicious, and we stood around the kitchen counter dipping shrimp and swapping stories.

"Since you don't drink, Dan, I'll pour you some sweet iced tea. Here have some." Martin handed me a tall cold glass. After a long and difficult day of riding, everything was tasting delicious. I began conversing with Ethan, and we went back and forth asking questions about each other's lives. After taking a few more sips of iced tea, I asked Martin where the bathroom was.

"Well, there is one upstairs with a shower, and one down here. You should really use the one down here though because I'm interested in what you'll think of my decorations," Martin said.

"What do you mean by decorations?" I asked.

"You'll see," he said with a smirk, pointing toward a door on the far side of the kitchen. I walked over, trying to guess what kind of "decorating" he meant. Maybe I would find portraits of Buddy dressed in a little doggy outfit or maybe a rainbow towel set. Frankly, I was expecting something colorful and artsy, the kind of thing that makes you smile and nod politely. I wasn't prepared for just how far his definition of décor was about to stretch.

As I cracked the door, the first thing that hit me was the color red. A dark velvet silk sheet hung from the ceiling like a theater curtain draped over the bathroom, and through the fabric dangled a reddish-yellow light fixture that looked like a Catholic censer that had been repurposed as a light. The walls, a patchwork of red and white, were studded with upside-down crucifixes in every conceivable size.

Paintings lined the walls of the room, along with shelves that held small sculptures of birds, animals, disoriented people, angels, demons, skeletons, and even a miniature Jesus. It looked like Martin had collected relics from all over the world and carefully arranged them in his bathroom. Mounted on the wall above the toilet was a narrow, red-stained wooden shrine that stretched from the top side of the toilet tank nearly to the ceiling. It wasn't very deep, but it had two delicate swinging doors that stayed opened revealing a mirror. Above the doors, several smaller mirrors were arranged in a dome shape, adding to its ornate design.

Sitting on top of the toilet tank, just in front of the shrine, were red candles held by an intricately carved eagle-dragon relic. On the lid of the toilet, right in the center, was a black circular sticker with an inverted pentagram around the head of a goat. The top two points of the star were the goat's horns, and the side points were its ears. The bottom point was its beard, and right in the center, its face and eyes gleamed at you. The pentagram represented the Church of Satan.

Before I could close the door, Martin called out from across the kitchen, "Along with being gay, I'm also a satanist, if that wasn't obvious."

Even though the bathroom wasn't that big, there was still more to take in. Against the wall, between the toilet and sink, stood a small red wooden pedestal with a square top, its edges adorned with carved drapery-like details. Its single leg curved like a serpent, but with wings, twisting down to its base in an eerie flowing design. On top of it sat a skull, a stone gargoyle glaring at me, and a large black book stamped with the same pentagram I'd already noticed on the toilet. *The Satanic Bible* seemed like an interesting choice for bathroom reading material.

Hanging above it all was a giant picture of a beast. The creature had a woman's body, goat's feet with legs tucked under a red blanket, and wings like that of something you'd see in a nightmare. Its goat head wore an upside-down pentagram on the forehead, and its beard hung between its bare chest with its arms pointed in two different directions, as if it were trying to confuse anyone playing charades. It was Baphomet, the so-called Sabbatic Goat. Since I hadn't closed the door to the bathroom yet, Martin asked, "What do you think?"

"It's a really interesting bathroom," I said.

"It's the one I have all my guests use. I love seeing their reactions," Martin said.

To me, it wasn't a big deal because I wasn't afraid of any of this, or of Martin. Some people are surprised when I say I wasn't scared to spend the night at his house, but I had no reason to be. That's because I'm confident in the words that the apostle John wrote, "He who is in you is greater than he who is in the world" (1 John 4:4).

After using the bathroom, I came out feeling relieved. As I walked through the kitchen, Martin wanted me to see all the pictures he had stuck on the refrigerator with magnets. "These are all of my ex-boyfriends," he said. The pictures were shots of different men posing with either a white muscle shirt or nothing but a prop covering themselves. "Cool," I responded, not really knowing what to say. "That guy looks like he was a character."

Martin laughed and then responded, "Oh, he was."

As I moved away from the fridge, Ethan said, "Pizza's here! Help yourself, Dan. We have plenty." I grabbed a slice and then sat down in the living room with the others.

Just as I was sinking into the coach with my first bite, Martin piped up, "So, Daniel here believes in God, so we're gonna have him pray to his God." The three of us paused mid-chew, exchanging surprised glances with each other, and then looked back at Martin to make sure we'd heard him correctly. For a moment, I couldn't tell if he was serious or just trying to be funny. Finally, I swallowed and asked, "How do you know I believe in God?"

Martin responded, "I read your Couchsurfing profile and saw that you're a Christian." (Actually, I hadn't explicitly stated that I was a Christian, but Martin made the correct assumption because I had used the words *faith* and *God* somewhere in my bio.) Martin added, "You know, I've never had a Christian stay at my house before, or at least not one that would admit to it." As Martin spoke, he stood up and walked to an end table beside the new sofa Chance was sitting on. From a small drawer, he retrieved a stack of small square papers. "I even got some prayer request cards here for us to write on," Martin said with sheer delight.

"Where did you get these from, Martin?" I asked in surprise.

"Oh, I stole them from a Catholic church years ago; I've been waiting to use them," he said as he began handing them out to the others. "Now, I want you guys to write down your prayer request on these cards, and then we're all going to have Dan pray for them." Ethan and Chance looked a bit confused and then expressed their reluctance to participate. Martin insisted, "Well, I just bought you guys pizza, so you have to do this."

They each accepted a card from Martin and together began jotting down prayer requests while I sat there waiting. Ethan and Chance had to think for a minute, but Martin got right to it. He quickly filled out one card and moved right on to the next and then another. By the time the others finished their first cards, Martin had filled out four. Then he collected the cards and handed them to me.

"Alright, here you go," Martin said as he placed the stack of cards in my hand. "You should read mine first. I'm excited to see what happens."

"OK," I said. "Well, I believe that God can hear everything I say, and He is listening to whatever I'm about to read. So, I'll just read them off like I'm talking to God." I picked up the first card written by Martin and read it aloud.

~~WORLD PEACE~~ (I JUST WANT THE AVOCADO PIT TO BE A LITTLE SMALLER.)

I showed the other guys that he had crossed out the words *WORLD PEACE*. Martin chuckled and then added, "I don't know why the avocado pit has to be so big. Wouldn't it be nice if it could be just a bit smaller?"

"Yeah, I guess that would be nice," I responded and then read his next request.

KILL ISIS!

After I read this out loud, I slowly looked up at Martin and then set it aside and proceeded to read the next one.

Exorcism on the electric outlets for Apt. # A3.

"Ah, sometimes that lamp flickers when it's plugged into that outlet. It's probably got a demon, right?" Martin said with a chuckle. I looked over at Ethan, who was rolling his eyes and shaking his head as I read the next one.

Smite A4!

This request referred to the neighbors who lived on the other side of the wall. Everyone looked over at Martin, as if we were searching for an explanation, when he said, "What? They can be really loud sometimes, especially at night, when Buddy and I are trying to sleep." Then I set his final card aside and read Chance's request to the group.

Make Kim Jong Un happy, so that North and South Korea can be friends.

"That's a good request," I commented. Then I read Ethan's card.

Please, help Daniel make it to San Francisco safely.

"Wow! Thanks, Bro! I really appreciate that."

"For sure, man," Ethan responded with a smile.

"So now that I've finished praying for all of *your* requests, do you mind if I pray my own?" I asked everybody. Ethan and Chance were fine with it, but Martin headed to the kitchen in a hurry, as if he was trying to get away. "Is that gonna be OK, Martin?" I called out.

"Umm, sure, I guess," he responded from the hallway. Maybe he thought I was going to pray fire down from heaven on him or something, but I simply began to speak prayers of blessing, peace, and love over the house and every individual in it. This approach aligns with Jesus's teachings to love those who disagree with you or those who act as your adversary, offering blessings instead of curses, and praying for those who mistreat you. Then I asked God to answer the requests according to His will and ended my prayer with the words, "In Jesus's name, let it be."

When I looked back at Martin, he radiated a new gentleness. In a calm tone, he said, "No one has ever prayed in my house before. Can I give you a hug?" I walked over and gave the satanist a hug. While my arms were around him, he said, "That was the most sincere thing I've ever heard." He patted my back and then told me, "You're welcome here anytime, and I'm sorry I walked away when you were about to pray."

"It's all good, Martin, and I appreciate you saying that. It means a lot," I responded with a smile.

Exhausted from a long day of riding, walking, and navigating through the vast Florida wilderness, I was eager to take a shower and sleep. I wished everyone a good night, and Martin showed me the upstairs bathroom. Chance bid us goodbye and departed, while Ethan retreated to his room. I refreshed myself with a warm shower and then returned downstairs to the distinctly themed satanic bathroom to brush my teeth. Martin provided me with a cozy blanket and pillow, and I nestled myself into the new living room couch and drifted into a peaceful sleep.

The next morning, Martin prepared a simple breakfast for us. When twelve o'clock rolled around, he generously offered to take me out for lunch. As we exited his apartment, he proudly gestured toward a striking white stone sculpture of a lion positioned by the front door. Since I had come in through the back door the night before, I hadn't seen the sculpture. The lion had dark black eyes and gripped a bone between its teeth, the tip of which was artfully painted red, hinting at a recent indulgence. Adorned around its neck was a metal chain that held a conspicuous sign with black letters boldly proclaiming, "SO MANY CHRISTIANS–SO FEW LIONS."

Martin pointed it out as we walked by. Because of how my name is associated with a lion's den, it made me chuckle. After lunch, I spent the day journaling, reading, and calling some friends. On February 28, 2018, I also shared an Instagram post about my time with Martin and posted a picture of him and Buddy posing next to the hungry lion sculpture on the front lawn. In that post, I included all six of the prayer requests. My memory escapes me on what we did for dinner, but I think Martin, Ethan, and I collaborated to make something delicious. Then I settled in for the second night on the orange couch.

The following day, I went on a walk around town with Martin and Buddy. Our return to A3 segued into an engrossing dialogue on God, religion, and philosophy. Martin would say that he was a satanist, but he also claimed to be an atheist. He once humorously described himself as a "gay, liberal, satanist atheist, who just so happens to be an artist." This self-professed title shed some light on his eclectic personality. He dismissed the existence of both Satan and God and viewed all religions with disdain. The purpose of his satanism was to antagonize Christians. His resentment stemmed from what he perceived as undue Christian influence pervading American culture and governance, exemplified by phrases like "In God We Trust" imprinted on US currency. Martin told me that the purpose of the Church of Satan, which he was a part of, was to counterbalance this dominance, asserting a parallel promotion of Satan, and that is what Martin had given his allegiance to.

Martin possessed a sharp intellect and eloquence that made our discussions both challenging and enlightening. Throughout our four-hour conversation that day, we delved deeper into our respective beliefs and even our upbringing and backgrounds. Our contrasting viewpoints kept us going back and forth, and Martin's expansive knowledge on various subjects made him a persuasive debater.

Whenever I admitted that I hadn't heard of a certain book he was referring to or some historical figure, he would say, "You have to enhance your intellectual toolbelt, Dan." I was only twenty-three at the time and far less educated than I could have been, so he was right about that. But then I began to push him on objective truth and the existence of a Creator.

Then Martin began speaking a little more intensely than he had before. "Believing in a god is a delusion. In fact, we can't really know if *anything* is objectively true or not. We need to embrace knowledge, hard work, and critical thinking to transcend this Christian America. Jesus didn't exist, and every point in the Bible contradicts itself. If after this conversation you go back to believing in the Bible and Christianity, you aren't being reasonable, and you won't progress very far in life. It's so sad to see such a humble, intelligent young man like you be so deceived. You've been brainwashed by your dad. The stuff he preached to you is a lie. I hope you call me up in ten years to tell me you've rejected all this nonsense."

As our conversation came to an end, I stood up and extended my hand to Martin, which he politely shook. We were still friendly with each other even though we had some foundational disagreements. We bid each other farewell as I walked out his front door and passed the lion one last time. I dropped my longboard, waved to Martin and Buddy, and skated away from A3.

The things Martin had said to me were fresh on my mind, and I began to question many of my fundamental beliefs. Doubts started creeping in as I replayed the conversation. I found myself wondering, *Do I really believe in God? Or am I delusional?* After fifteen minutes of mentally debating myself, I remembered that statement Martin had made: "You can't really know if *anything* is objectively true." I began to replay this phrase in my head, carefully dissecting each word, and thought, *Wait a minute. That statement contradicts itself. It defies the Law of Non-Contradiction.* He was saying that *nothing* is absolutely true while claiming that his statement was absolutely true. But *nothing* means no thing. So how can someone believe that something is objectively true while saying that nothing is objectively true? To me, that's delusional. It's like saying, "Words don't exist," while you use three words to make your point.

While Martin urged me to be a strong and critical thinker about *my* beliefs, it struck me that he probably wasn't critically examining his own beliefs. It raises the question of how one can advocate for knowledge, hard work, and critical thinking without embracing the most fundamental principle of all knowledge—truth. If there is no truth, then he himself cannot definitively determine the ultimate truth of his own beliefs. He cannot be confident in anything he believes because he doesn't believe that *anything* is ultimately true. It's like constructing a house on a foundation of sand; while it may look nice or appear sturdy, it's destined to crumble under pressure, and if your beliefs can't withstand pressure, why would you want to believe them?

For these reasons, I decided that he wasn't offering me anything better than what I already had, so I went on trusting in Jesus, who claimed to be "the Truth" and then validated his claim by rising from the dead after being crucified by Romans. I know that seems crazy and unscientific to believe, but it's arguably one of the most reliable historical events that has ever occurred in human history. Martin would laugh at this statement, and that's fine. But think about this: You can visit the tomb of Muhammad in Saudi Arabia. You can walk the grounds of Confucius's cemetery in China. You can stand before the Taj Mahal, the resting place of Mumtaz Mahal, or see the mummies in the great pyramids of Egypt that were buried in gold. But what's the difference between the tomb of Jesus in Jerusalem and all the others? His tomb is empty. And that changes everything. If you want to explore this more, I highly recommend the book, *More Than a Carpenter* by Josh McDowell.

Although I thought Martin and his dog, Buddy, were great hosts, after I left, we didn't stay in touch. For me, I just continued on the longboard heading west. A few months later, my friend Jesse shared some international news with me that left me stunned. *The Guardian* published an article featuring a picture of North and South Korea's leaders shaking hands. The headline read, "Korean leaders bond over handshakes and 'a lot of pictures.' Korea summit's positive mood appears to break 65 years of North and South animosity." The article was dated April 27, 2018, exactly two months since the prayer requests were made. But God didn't stop there.

At some point during my trip, I cut open a big Hass avocado and found a small pit inside. It reminded me of Martin's first prayer request. I wonder what would have happened if he hadn't crossed out ~~"WORLD PEACE"~~.

In October of 2018, eight months after the prayers, Hurricane Michael left a trail of devastation in Panama City. It was a Category 5 storm, and 500,000 people were told to evacuate immediately. Satellite images vividly depicted the striking contrast of Panama City before and after Hurricane Michael. I became curious about the destruction when I started noticing a pattern of answered prayers to the six requests initiated by Martin.

I distinctly remember that Martin requested unit A4 to be smote. When I located it online, I zoomed in on apartment A4 and noticed a large and mysterious piece of white debris laying off the back side of apartment A4. The hurricane seemed to have obliterated the entire back two-story deck, along with a big wall. I am simply stating the facts, not offering explanations. Martin asked for A4 to be smote, and then a hurricane tore the deck and back wall away. And, I think if there were any demons in A3's electrical outlets, they weren't there anymore.

After doing this research and seeing the results of this prayer request, I felt compelled, while writing this book, to investigate ISIS. Although I had heard that the US government had claimed to have eliminated ISIS, I was unaware of when it happened. I looked it up and found that the U.S. conducted a military operation on October 26 to 27, 2019, during which the leader of ISIS was killed.

This shocked me because October 26, 2019, marked my twenty-fifth birthday, and on October 27, I achieved my coast-to-coast goal of longboarding across America. Although I continued on to San Francisco, October 27 was the day I jumped into the Pacific Ocean at Huntington Beach, California. I know it sounds like unbelievable timing, but this is what happened.

The final prayer request was answered on December 7, 2019, when I finally made it to San Francisco's Golden Gate Bridge. I had never seen the bridge in person, but when I did, I was taken aback by how big it was. The bridge looked spectacular, and I was stoked to be there. Then I took a video, explaining how I was surprised by the fact that it never rained on me the entire trip, not one time. Sometimes I would be on the longboard for about nine or ten hours a day, but it wouldn't ever rain while I was riding. The times it did rain, I was always at somebody's house staying dry and warm.

When I reached the bridge, my old college friend Luke, who lived in San Francisco, was there to congratulate me and capture some pictures. As we stood there taking pictures, suddenly it began to downpour. I pulled out my phone to capture the moment with another video, and then we made our way to a small café adjacent to the bridge so we could get out of the rain. When we got there, we looked back at the iconic landmark and were treated to the beautiful sight of a massive rainbow arching over the top of the Golden Gate Bridge.

When the rainbow came out, I exclaimed, "Oh my God!" because He is truly incredible. He didn't forget about the prayer request that I would arrive safely to my end destination. The rainbow felt like a divine seal of completion. In Genesis 9, God created the rainbow as a promise to mankind that He would never destroy the whole world with a flood ever again. God always keeps His promises.

Another promise God has made to us is that if we ask *anything* according to the name of Jesus, He will do it. If there is one thing I've learned about prayer through all this, it's that the word "anything" really means anything. I used to imagine that God only answered the prayers of the faithful churchgoer, but now I believe that God can answer the prayers of a satanist too. He is never late, rarely early, and always on time. And if He can answer the prayers of a satanist, He can answer yours too. You just have to ask.

So, you want to know what "Love and Longboard" means to me? It was the purpose statement of my entire trip, to longboard across America and love everyone along the way. It's what I've learned from Jesus; it's what I've learned from God. It means being patient and kind, not being selfish or rude. Take it from my future good friend Bob Goff, who said it this way in his book *Everybody, Always* (2018): "Love isn't something we fall into; love is someone we become. [...] We might be known for our opinions, [but] we'll be remembered for our love." Anyone can be patient and kind with their friends, and maybe even their family; that's pretty easy. But Jesus taught us to love our enemies too. That means the difficult, disagreeable, and creepy ones; that even means the satanist who lives in A3.

CHAPTER 2.

A $15,000 STORY

1994 – 2020

I used to imagine that generosity only impacted the person who received, but now I believe it creates a ripple effect that touches countless lives.

Growing up, life was pretty good; it wasn't perfect, but the truth is, I wasn't either. We were seven kids under one roof, which meant chaos came with the furniture. I think my siblings would agree that I received the most discipline out of all of us. I was a bit of a rebel, probably more than a bit. Ironically, my dad's career was Christian ministry, and we kids made sure that he was good at it. My mom's career was in childhood education, and she spent her days homeschooling all of us while taking care of the newest baby.

I hate to say it now, but we did not make it easy on her. One time, my younger brother and I caught a goldfinch. We had trapped it in our garage, and then I quickly grabbed it before it could fly away. Its wings fluttered frantically against the palms of my hands as I tried to make sure it didn't escape. I marveled at its bright yellow feathers and delicate features. Its breast was warm, and I could feel its heartbeat rapidly pulsing against my fingertips. I thought it was the coolest thing ever, and I just had to show my mom. In my little head, I was convinced that she would be very proud of her son who caught such a beautiful bird.

She was inside taking a nap because, well, the baby and all. We could have waited for her to wake up, but this was far more important than sleeping. So, we quietly walked into her bedroom and gently said, "Mom, guess what we caught?" Well, she was fast asleep and couldn't hear us. So, I held the bird with one hand and used the other hand to wake her up. As I loosened my grip, that sneaky, little bird immediately escaped and started flying around the room like a maniac just as my mom opened her eyes from a deep sleep. Needless to say, she didn't have quite the reaction I was imagining.

My childhood was anything but normal. Our family moved around a lot; that's probably how I got my wanderlust. By the time I was fifteen years old, we had moved about once every three years. My dad was an Independent Fundamental Baptist pastor. If you don't know what that means, it's OK. I'm still not quite sure myself. But he was always switching jobs, and I was really good at packing up my stuff. I think moving was our family's spiritual gift. From my point of view as a child, every new church came with a new zip code and a new set of rules.

The regulations around music, hairstyles, my attire, and what version of the Bible was the right one changed with every church we attended. It was a challenge to keep track of what was moral and what was "sinful." But the most important thing was always making sure you went to church. We went on Sunday mornings, Sunday nights, Wednesday evenings, and sometimes even on Saturdays to clean the building. As a kid, I believed in God, but I didn't *know* Him. He was a distant figure, a ticket out of hell when I died. "Save me," I'd pray night after night while I lay in bed. I was just making sure God knew I didn't want to go to that terrible place. It was a shallow understanding of salvation. I see now that the churches we attended taught me religion, not relationship. They taught me to follow the rules but didn't teach me much about knowing God intimately and walking in relationship with Him. I hadn't experienced the boundless love of my heavenly Father yet.

When I was fifteen, our family moved to Iowa, where my dad became a senior pastor, and I became a secret rebel. I learned how to tell my parents and the people at church what they wanted to hear. But I would sneak out at night to do things I shouldn't have been doing. I was so good at living a double life that my parents never caught me. Yes, pastors' kids can sometimes be the worst ones, and I'm not proud of that. I look back now and see all the growth opportunities I missed out on because I had no relationship with God.

Growing up, I made plenty of mistakes. I wish I could go back and do things differently. The hard reality is that we don't get a second chance. We all have been given a single life to live. It doesn't take long to learn that you can't change your past, but as I longboarded 3,200 miles through eight states and many cities, I began to believe in a new reality—you can change your future, and if you do it with God, it will be even better than you can imagine.

When I was seventeen, my dad wanted me to attend a Bible college in northern Wisconsin called Northland. I reluctantly honored my dad's wish and agreed to attend for at least one year. After that first year of Bible college, I had no plans of returning to Northland or my parents' house because I didn't like all the rules. Growing up in the church, our youth pastor told us not to drink, smoke or chew, or date girls who do. Well, those are the exact things my curious self began to explore. That summer was my first summer of freedom away from anyone telling me what I could and couldn't do. It had its ups and downs, and as much as I learned from it, none of that stuff made my life feel any more meaningful. On top of that, it was clear that I hadn't made many good decisions.

Feeling a bit lost, I began to search for some guidance. I ended up asking my best friend Tristan to go with me to a Sunday morning church service that some of our friends attended. The pastor told a story of how his family traveled to a faraway country to adopt a young girl who had no parents; she was living in an orphanage that sat in the middle of a city filled with crime, violence, and poverty. He explained that they had to fly to one country where they waited several hours for a flight to another country and then took a bus several more hours to the impoverished city. Then they had to fill out paperwork and wait. As I sat there wondering what on earth would motivate someone to go through all that trouble for one little girl, he said these words: "The love that I have for our new daughter is the same love that God the Father has for me."

That blew me away; I couldn't stop thinking about those words. It made me feel like there was something about God's love that I didn't quite understand. Even though I was the son of a pastor, had been to Bible school, and had sat through hundreds of church services by that time, I still had never heard anything like that. I guess I didn't have the ears to hear, but the words he spoke that morning hit me differently than anything before. It was like a light flipped on in my head that lit up a new perspective of God and His love.

When I got back in Tristan's car, we talked about God and the story of the orphan. I remember saying this in my heart: *OK, God, I can see that there is more to You than I thought. I'll go back to Northland for another year to see what I can learn and give You a second chance.* It was the end of August. School was starting soon, so I signed back up for classes and went back to Bible college.

A couple of months into the school year, things were going well, but I found myself stranded at my friend Josiah's house one Sunday afternoon. I needed to get back to campus, but he couldn't drive me without being late for work. I couldn't find anyone to pick me up because I was twenty-one miles from campus. Then a wild idea came into my mind. I looked at Josiah and said to him, "Maybe I'll just try to longboard back to campus." I had my longboard with me and plenty of time before dinner. "What's the worst that could happen?" I asked.

Josiah raised his eyebrows and said, "Well, that's pretty far, Bro, but I believe you can make it. I mean, you don't really have any other good option right now."

And just like that, the day after my nineteenth birthday on a beautiful October afternoon, I started my first long-distance longboarding excursion. There was a light wind, no humidity, with golden sunlight shining in my face. I was listening to "Say Hey (I Love You)" by Michael Franti through my earbuds and cruising down Highway 141. I was longboarding on the shoulder of the road and was thankful for how smooth it was.

I began to wonder if any highway patrol officers would stop me. A few passed by but didn't seem to care. After the first twelve miles, I was still feeling great. Then I thought, *I wonder how far I could make it on this board. Maybe I could longboard all the way to Green Bay. That'd be cool! Or what if I kept going and made it all the way to Chicago? Dang, how sick would that be!* Then the thought that changed my entire life popped into my head for the first time: *What if I longboarded across America—coast to coast?*

My eyes widened, and a big smile came across my face. "That would be INSANE but so freaking amazing!" I said to no one in particular. Then I looked down and took another push with my foot on the longboard and felt more of that Wisconsin breeze against my face. My imagination ran wild as I thought of all the crazy adventures a trip like that could offer. I immediately envisioned myself traveling from the Atlantic Ocean to the Pacific. *I would meet so many people,* I thought. *And I would have stories to talk about for the rest of my life.*

Sometimes we underestimate just how powerful our thoughts can be. But I've come to realize that every great accomplishment begins in the imagination. Our minds shape ideas into words, and those words become the starting point that brings our dreams to life. Our words are so influential. Don't forget about Proverbs 18, which says that "Death and life are in the power of the tongue." The easiest way to kill a dream is to talk about how it won't work. Speak life to a dream by talking about how it will succeed, and the odds are better that it will.

I didn't waste any time transforming my new dream into words. I started telling my closest friends about this ambitious idea of mine, but only my closest friends because I didn't want people speaking death to my dream. I was determined to see it through. I was excited to get going, but two big things were holding me back. First, I wanted to graduate college because I was determined to finish what I'd started. Secondly, I wanted to pay off my student loans because I didn't want to travel with a bunch of debt hanging over my head. Now that I had a dream and two big goals toward achieving that dream, my mind was laser-focused.

The idea of longboarding coast to coast had popped into my mind during the fall of my sophomore year at Northland. While I was in Milwaukee for the following Christmas break, a series of events began to unfold that made me believe, for the first time, that to love God meant to love others. It started when I went to breakfast with my new friend Tim and listened to him talk about how God was using him to simply love the people around him. It was like *that light* that had been flipped on in my head was turning on a flame in my heart—a passion to love God by loving others. For the first time, I trusted that God was sovereign over my life and wanted what was best for me. As I drove back home from breakfast, I told God, "I'll start doing whatever You want me to do." From then on, it felt like we were friends, and my life drastically changed. When I came back to college from Christmas break, everyone at school knew I was a completely different person.

I continued studying at the school, and while I was at Northland, I began experiencing many things that increased my faith in God. However, just before my final year at the university, the school suddenly closed. In order to finish my degree, I had to transfer to another school. I chose Lancaster Bible College (LBC) in Pennsylvania. Transferring in as a senior made me feel like a freshman again. Fortunately, I became great friends with my new admissions counselor, Kim Metzler, who had kids my age. After I told her about my crazy ambition to go on this longboard trip, she became my biggest fan and a great mentor to me as well. Kim believed in me. She would always check up on me and pray for my well-being. She helped me find purpose when I felt unsure and even met up with me while I was on my longboard trip. No one else made such a supportive effort as Kim did, and for that, I am grateful.

In May 2016, I graduated from LBC but had racked up $23,000 dollars of debt. On top of that, I needed to move out of the campus dorm I had been living in, so Kim came to the rescue and connected me with her parents, who were retired and lived about twenty minutes away. Gammy and Pa agreed to host me in a small room located on the second floor of their home for the summer, but it actually turned out to be nine months. While I was there, they found out about my weak financial situation and signed me up for Dave Ramsey's Financial Peace University.

Every week, Gammy and Pa would drive me to class and sit with me through the whole thing. During this class, I realized that it would take me up to four years to pay back my loans, if I was diligent. This hit me like a ton of bricks because I desperately wanted to get going on my longboard journey. Then this Bible verse popped into my head: With God all things are possible. I thought about it for a while, especially the words "all things." For some reason, I just couldn't help but wonder if the verses really meant what it said. Then I thought of something radical, something that seemed impossible. "OK, God," I prayed. "Since all things are possible for You, can You please get me out of debt in one day?"

I was asking God to remove $23,000 of student loans in a single day. I was filled with anticipation at what God might do that evening, but I received no phone calls, no letters, and no surprise emails from any rich relative. I went to sleep with hope in my heart but woke up the next day with nothing.

Did God say no? I wondered. *Maybe I need to ask Him again?* I had heard the Bible story of the widow who kept pestering a judge by asking him for justice, and eventually he gave her what she asked for. This inspired me to be more persistent with God.

A year later, I still had debt. But I had paid off $8,000 with all the extra money I made from my job. I had also moved out of Gammy and Pa's house in Pennsylvania and moved in with my younger cousin, Justin Matthews, in South Carolina. Justin worked in a restaurant, and I worked pouring concrete. I was still putting money toward paying off my debt, and Justin was really good at saving money. He knew I wouldn't start my longboard trip until I was debt-free.

One morning, while Justin and I were enjoying some coffee, he asked, "Hey, how much debt do you have left?"

"Around $15,000," I responded.

"Hmm…" Justin paused for a second and then continued, "Well, this morning I felt God bring to my mind that I should pay off your debt, and it just so happens that I have a little over $15,000 in my savings account." I paused and thought, *There's no way!*

When I asked God to get me out of debt in a single day, I imagined that some wealthy person would call me up and tell me they were going to pay off my student loans, not my cousin. He's four years younger than me and had been working hard at a low-paying job while saving every dime he could. It was truly impressive that he had saved this much money at such a young age, as he was only eighteen.

When Justin said that God was leading him to give me almost all his savings, I thought, *No way!* "Are you joking?" I asked. At first, I couldn't tell if Justin was being serious because he loves to joke around.

Then he said, "I've talked to my mentor and have prayed long and hard about it. I feel this is what God wants me to do."

So, Justin decided he was going to pay off my debt.

Sure enough, on Friday, September 8, 2017, he took $8,000 cash from a safe in his bedroom to the bank and deposited it into my account. Then he wired me another $7,000. He told me he didn't expect me to pay him back; it was a free gift, and I only had to receive it. I can't tell you how good it felt to have $15,000 of debt wiped clean in a single day. When my head hit the pillow that night, I realized that God had done the impossible. He answered my persistent prayers.

When I look back on that day, I realize it changed everything for me. It shifted how I thought about my possessions, my money, and especially the power of prayer. Now whenever it seems like there's no way, I remind myself that there's Yahweh.

At this point, I had been talking about my dream to cross America for four years. Now that I had finished college and my debt was paid, I began preparing for my journey. I gave away everything I owned to friends, family, and people in need. My plan was to drive down to Florida, sell my car, and start longboarding west from the Atlantic Ocean. I took a circuitous route to Florida, stopping at friends' and families' houses along the way and thanking everyone in person who had supported my dream from the beginning, and I'm really glad I did.

After a few months of traveling around in my car, I finally drove past the famous WELCOME TO FLORIDA: THE SUNSHINE STATE sign. My windows were down, and I was vibing to the song "King Without a Crown" by Matisyahu. My face brightened as the warm air blasted through the cabin of my car. I took a deep breath of satisfaction, knowing how far I had come; it was the second time in my life that I had passed that sign. Back in 2014, I had done a test run trip, traveling on my longboard east across the southern part of Florida from Naples to Miami. During that trip, I had made some good friends in Miami, which is why I decided to start my journey there.

It was now January 2018, and I was on my way to Ric's place. He owned a house on the west side of Miami where he, his wife, and daughters lived. They were the ones I had met during my first trip to Florida and were offering to host me again while I was in town. After a lot of driving, I finally arrived in front of their house with an empty tank of gas and a total of $0.27 to my name. I couldn't have driven any further, even if I wanted to. I was completely broke, so it felt like I was in the exact spot that I was supposed to be. When I turned off the car, I didn't even think it would start again.

Ric and his wife, Gloria, hugged me once I got out of my car. "It's so good to see you, Daniel," Gloria said. "We're so glad you made it all the way here."

"How was the trip? Long?" Ric asked. "Did you have good weather?"

"Have you eaten anything?" Gloria interrupted. "Are you hungry? We picked up some food for you on our way back from church. Come and eat with us!" They made me feel right at home. I greeted their daughters, Sarah and Annita, with a hug and kiss in the Miami-Latino way.

They lived in a large two-story stucco home in a Miami suburb; its arched portico and eight columns gave it a Spanish flare. A curved paver driveway led to the entrance framed by neatly trimmed hedges, while towering palm trees watched over the property. Behind the house, a bright blue swimming pool was surrounded by a patio area with outdoor seating and a grill, perfect for hosting gatherings. Their home served as a place of ministry, especially for those coming from southern countries. The whole property had the warm, polished look of a well-kept Florida home. I don't remember them having any pets, just the usual street cats that roamed the neighborhood, slipping between cars and lounging in the driveway like they owned the place.

As we sat down at the family dining room table, we enjoyed some delicious fajitas along with some great conversation. Gloria had prepared a nice bedroom for me and told me that I was welcome to stay as long as I needed. I wanted to start the journey as soon as possible, but first, I had to sell my car.

Without money and gas, I wasn't sure what I was going to do. I didn't want to ask anyone for money, so I began to ask God to provide some for me. The next day I saw a guy mowing a lawn and asked him for a job, but he didn't speak English. I couldn't stay with Ric and Gloria forever, but I had no idea what to do. A couple of days went by, and a letter came in the mail with my name on it. My mom had sent me a nice card with $30 dollars inside. It came at the perfect time.

That afternoon, I tried to start my car, and it fired right up! I drove it to the nearest gas station, filled it up, and washed it. I wanted to use the vacuum, but I needed ten more cents. So, I prayed, "God, you know my needs and faithfully provide. Please give me the ten cents I need to vacuum my car." When I looked up, there across the parking lot was a small, silver coin. It was a dime!

After vacuuming my car, I took it to a local dealer that offered me fourteen hundred dollars for it, and that's how much money I had at the beginning of my trip. It felt like more than enough money for my journey because I knew my heavenly Dad would provide for all my needs just like He had already done time and time again.

Throughout the trip across America, I did my best to be radically generous by giving what I could to others along the way. When I was about halfway through Florida, I decided to sponsor some African children living in extreme poverty and haven't quit to this day. Another time, a friend from college messaged me on Facebook asking to support their coffee cart ministry. I sent her $100 several weeks into my longboard trip when money was tight for me. There was another time I felt God leading me to send another $100 to two friends who were on a faith journey going from Oklahoma to South Carolina. I really didn't want to send this money because I felt I needed it, but I couldn't get away from the promptings of the Holy Spirit, and my friends really appreciated me doing that.

I did my best to keep my hands open so that I could give and receive whatever God wanted me to. If it weren't for people like Justin in my life who showed me what radical generosity looked like, I'm not sure I would be so willing to give. It's easy to give $100 when you're a millionaire, but when you only have a three-digit bank account, it hits differently.

There was a moment in the middle of my trip when I felt God prompting me not just to give a percentage of the money I had, but to give it all. I didn't have more than forty dollars in my bank account at the time, so I was already stretched thin, especially with my monthly phone bill always sneaking up on me. That week, I took a job installing LVP flooring in a small rental house to help supplement my income on the road. I made $500 from the job and was paid on Friday. That same evening, I stood beside my friend Kevin as he grilled meat for dinner, listening to him talk about his upcoming mission trip to the Philippines. He needed a few thousand dollars to go. As he spoke, I felt a clear nudge from God to give him the money I had just made.

Rationally, it made no sense; I needed that money for my phone bill. My right shoe had a hole in the bottom of it and was slowly growing bigger with each step. But I knew what God had put in my heart to do. Without hesitation, I handed over the $500 dollars to Kevin. I didn't resist; I just gave it all away.

There was another time when two homeless guys needed clothes in New Mexico, so I let them grab whatever they needed from what I had. They ended up taking it all, and I just let them because I wanted to experience what it was like to be so radically generous that you give away everything you own.

In all these moments, I actually gained more than I gave away. I gained a deeper understanding of my true needs and God's provision. Whether I have $15,000 dollars in my hands or nothing, I could still be secure and joyful knowing that my contentment is not based on what I have but on the love that God has for me. Romans 5:8 says, "God demonstrates His own love toward us, in that while we were still sinners, Christ died for us." And the apostle John recorded Jesus saying that whoever believes in Him will have eternal life and will have it abundantly (John 3 and John 10).

God loves it when we step out in faith and trust Him to provide for our needs, and He does provide. In every one of those situations, God returned the favor to me. People gave me more money along the way, someone else bought me nice clothes, and another guy sent me money to buy a new pair of shoes. This last one is hard to believe, but in the middle of my trip, I even had a friend sign over the title to his really nice 2004 Harley Davidson Sportster. The cool thing was that I never asked anyone for any of these things. Most of them responded that they were giving me something because God had laid it on their hearts. If you don't believe in God, maybe my stories will help you understand why I've decided to put my trust in Him.

When I finished the trip across America, I couldn't stop thinking about all the kindness and generosity I experienced along the way. It was hard to get over the fact that my younger cousin paid off my college debt when he hadn't even gone to college himself. So, I asked God if He wanted me to give Justin a gift of money. After completing my journey, I moved to Washington State and built tiny homes with Handcrafted Movement, saving every penny I could. After six months, I had a little over $15,000.

During the summer of 2020, I rode my Harley 23,000 miles around the United States, and when I rode through South Carolina, I went out to breakfast with Justin. He was about to propose to his girlfriend, Mary. I was so excited for him, and then I asked him about his financial situation, and he told me, "Last year, when I started my lawn business, I had to take out a big loan. I've been paying it off ever since, and right now I have about $15,000 of debt left to pay." I was shocked. It was the exact amount he had given me and the exact amount I had in savings. The tables had turned; I had no doubt God was answering my question about giving a gift of money to Justin.

After breakfast, Justin resumed mowing lawns while I rode my motorcycle over to the bank. I headed to the bank and requested a $15,000 check from the teller. Once I received the check, I rode to Justin's house. Although he wasn't home, I found the side door unlocked and entered. I left the $15,000 dollar check with his name on it and wrote, "Thanks for taking a step of faith," and placed it in the sock drawer of his nightstand next to his bed. It was Thursday, August 20, 2020. The next time I saw Justin, he gave me the most heartfelt hug I've ever received. We couldn't stop smiling as we savored the moments of joy of both giving and receiving.

Generosity has a ripple effect. It not only inspires those who experience it, but also those who hear its stories. Maybe this story has impacted you in some way. It encourages me to have radical faith and always be willing to give a little more generously than what is normal. You may not feel led to give $15,000 dollars, but I encourage you to listen to the Spirit of God and do whatever He wants because He knows what's best. Giving in faith doesn't just mean giving away your money either. There are other ways to give. You can be generous with your time, your talents, your words, and other things.

Generosity is about trusting God to do more than we can see. What if the whole world became a little more generous? It takes a lot of faith to give everything, but we all can give at least something. Through all this, I've learned one thing to be true: *If you want to live in faith—give in faith.* God can start a ripple effect of generosity and touch countless lives with those who are willing to listen and obey.

CHAPTER 3.

DIVINE ENCOUNTERS

JANUARY 18 – FEBRUARY 4, 2018
MIAMI TO SARASOTA, FLORIDA

I used to imagine that doing the illogical was reckless, but now I believe that sometimes it's God's strategy for divine encounters.

Right before embarking on my journey across the United States, I found myself gripped in a conversation with a close friend. We were going back and forth about what items would be essential for traveling across the country. "Bro, you're longboarding across America," he said. "You have to bring a tent!" The idea of venturing without any sleeping gear had been rolling around in my head for a few months, and I just couldn't push that thought away.

My friend's genuine care for my well-being and his logical argument almost convinced me. However, in the thick of our discussion, I couldn't shake an inexplicable, persistent inner voice nudging me to trust God and not bring the gear. *But what if I can't find a place to sleep?* I thought. *What if I get rained on? What if I have to sleep outside?* I countered. I confess the idea of traveling without a tent made me nervous because I knew I wouldn't have enough money to buy myself a bunch of hotel rooms along the way. But because I had learned to recognize the still, small voice of God within my heart, I knew that this thought to venture without the sleeping gear was actually a prompting from the Spirit of Jesus.

The book of John says that Jesus is the Good Shepherd, and His sheep hear His voice. Sometimes He persuades me to do something that defies all reason, but it's precisely at those moments when your feet are on the edge of a proverbial cliff and that taking a leap of faith will bring about the greatest adventures. Embracing this belief, I put my trust in the still, small voice and summoned the courage to take the first push of faith on my longboard heading west without any sleeping gear. My heart filled with a mixture of nerves and excitement as I embarked on this extraordinary adventure, armed with nothing more than a small backpack, a leather Bible, and my trusty longboard. I was trusting that God would provide a place for me to stay each night along the way.

↩

On Thursday, January 18, 2018, I woke up in the guest bedroom at Ric and Gloria's house. The sun was already beaming down, warming the cool Floridian air. The forecast predicted a high of 72 degrees, and the sky was a peaceful shade of light blue, making it the ideal day to begin my long-awaited longboarding excursion. My car was sold, and I had enough cash to last me about a couple of months. I grabbed my longboard and was ready to go.

Ric was an officer for the Miami-Dade Police Department, and he had agreed to drive me to Miami Beach before work. So, at 6 a.m., I hopped into his squad car, and he whisked me away to the beach. It was like getting a police escort on the first day of my adventure. The plan was to touch the Atlantic Ocean, take some pictures, and then longboard twenty-five miles back to Ric's house. Soon we arrived just a few hundred feet from the beach: I stepped out of the squad car, thanked him for the ride, and waved to him as he drove away.

I walked onto the soft, sandy shore of Miami Beach, where the Atlantic stretched endlessly to my left. The beach was wide and welcoming, with clear turquoise water rolling in gentle waves. Behind me, the high-rises of Miami Beach towered over the shoreline, while to my right, the pier buzzed with fishermen and tourists taking in the view. The sun was beginning to rise higher in the sky, casting a golden glow over the sand. It was the perfect place to mark the start of my journey, standing at the edge of the continent.

Finally, I thought to myself, *after four years, my dream has now become a reality.* I carried my longboard across the sand to the waves. I touched the wheels in the ocean water, took a deep breath, and snapped a picture to document the moment. Then I saw South Pointe Pier in the distance and walked all the way to the edge of it. That's when I met Johnny and longboarded back down the pier with him saying, "San Francisco, here I come!"

My trip had officially begun. As I cruised down the boardwalk past all the gigantic Miami buildings, I kept looking at them as they seemed to smoothly move across the blue sky. I had to be careful not to stare too long or else I might run into someone because the area was packed with people walking, jogging, and riding all sorts of wheeled things. The canal was filled with boats and cruise ships floating over the calm waters. As I went, I called a few friends and family to tell them that I had just started my trip across the United States of America. Everyone was so excited for me.

I embarked on this journey fully aware that it would consume at least a year of my life, if not longer, but I didn't have any predetermined end date. With minimal financial obligations and a profound trust in God to provide, I gave up any sense of urgency. I believed wholeheartedly that God would meet all my needs along the way. Well, it was easy to believe in His provision at that moment because I had a warm and inviting bed waiting for me at Ric's house, but the days to follow would be a real test of faith.

As I traveled, I used Google Maps navigation and set it to the bicycle option, which kept me off the busiest roads. Miami, like most big cities I longboarded through, had smooth, well-maintained bike paths that made skating effortless. That day felt almost too easy: the sun was shining, the pavement was perfect, and I barely had to think about where I was going. I weaved past cyclists and joggers, the city humming around me, but all I really remember is how beautiful and smooth the ride was.

I made it back to Ric's house well before the sun dipped below the horizon, and the whole family congratulated me on completing my first day. Given my lack of urgency, I decided to stay for the weekend so I could say goodbye to the friends I had made at their church. After a beautiful Sunday night worship service and a round of heartfelt hugs and friendly kisses from everyone saying goodbye, I got back to Ric's around 9 p.m. I went straight to bed because I had plans to leave early the following morning to make it to the southwest coast of Naples.

I woke up more excited than I'd ever been on a Monday. Ric got up with me and met me in the kitchen to bid me farewell. "Take this, Daniel," he said, pressing a hundred-dollar bill in my hand. "You can buy yourself a place to stay at a hotel tonight." I gave Ric a huge hug and could feel my faith growing and my nerves calming at the thought of not having to sleep outside. That day, I longboarded eighty miles from the outskirts of Miami to the southern edge of Naples, located on the west side of the Florida Peninsula. It took me twelve hours to cross the Everglades on Highway 41. Along the way, I thought a lot about all the planning I had done for the past four years. As night fell, I booked a small room at a motel in Naples with the money Ric gave me. Finally, I took a nice shower and got ready for bed. The second day on the longboard was completed, but I was dead tired and immediately fell fast asleep on the bed.

It was now Tuesday morning. I woke up aching, my body sore from the miles behind me. I wanted to sleep longer, but the road was calling. Stephanie, a dear friend, and her daughter, Lily, were waiting for me at their house in south Fort Myers just off Highway 41, where they would host me for the night. Our paths had first crossed four years earlier during that test trip I took across Florida.

I went to Florida in 2014 during my college Christmas break. I took this trip to share the love of Jesus and prepare for my journey across America by testing what it would be like to longboard in a state I had never been. This led me to my original encounter with Ric and his family in Miami, and also Stephanie in Fort Myers. My encounter with these people felt divinely orchestrated, especially Stephanie.

Raised in the occult, Stephanie had been reading tarot cards by the age of seven, surrounded by crystal ball readers in her family. She eventually became a practicing witch before encountering Jesus, who had been pursuing her all along. By the time I met her, she had just escaped from an abusive husband and was living with her grandmother, walking to work every day to support her one-year-old daughter. Three days before I met Stephanie, she had begun fasting and crying out to God, desperate for something real, pleading for a sign that He heard her prayers.

Then, on December 22, 2014, I longboarded up to the Taco Bell in Fort Myers where she worked, just before they closed that night. Tired and hungry, I sat down to charge my phone and eat tacos. The workers noticed me because I stood out with my small backpack and longboard, but it was Stephanie who struck up a conversation with me while mopping the floor near my table. We talked for a while and when her shift ended late that night, that persistent, inner voice said to me, *Ask if you can walk her home.* I felt weird asking a stranger if I could walk her home, but somehow, she trusted me and said yes.

"So, what are you doing in Florida?" she asked.

"I'm on a faith journey with Jesus," I responded.

"You're a Christian too?" Stephanie asked excitedly. Then she told me she had been studying the book of Daniel and was in the middle of a Daniel Fast, which meant she was only eating plant-based foods. To her, the fact that my name was Daniel felt like confirmation. While we sat on the curb outside her apartment complex, I played "Somewhere Over the Rainbow" on the ukulele that I had been carrying with me during this test trip. Stephanie was caught off guard and deeply moved—this was the song she sang to Lily every night before bed. To her, it felt like another confirmation that God was communicating with her. Then, we said our goodbyes, and I longboarded away into the night.

We hadn't exchanged contact info, so we lost touch for several months, but then we finally reconnected through Facebook. Stephanie told me, "For the longest time, I was convinced that you were an angel because when you longboarded away, it was as if you suddenly vanished. And that night I played the song 'Oceans' by Hillsong while I fell asleep and had a dream that I was walking on the water with Jesus."

Stephanie had been fasting because she was asking God for a sign that He was with her through the struggles she was facing. She was so encouraged from our meeting that she posted about it on Facebook and told her pastor. Stephanie tried to make sense of it all but deep down, she knew; it was the moment she needed, the reminder that she wasn't going to sink. God made Himself real to her that night by saying, "You're not going to sink. You're gonna walk on water. I won't let you go."

It had now been four years since that night, and we were about to reconnect. Once they opened their door, Stephanie and Lily's warm embrace made me feel welcome once again. They fed me and offered me a nice couch for me to sleep on. The following morning, Stephanie and her grandmother gathered around me to pray before I set off.

Stephanie anointed my forehead with Cedar of Lebanon oil, explaining that, like those trees, I would grow steadily and strong in the Lord, able to withstand the winds and storms ahead. She reminded me that cedars thrive on mountaintops, close to God, just as I was setting out on a journey of faith, solely trusting in Him. With her hands on my shoulders, she prayed for angels to surround and protect me, speaking blessings over my mission like the Prayer of Jabez. When Stephanie began to pray in tongues, I felt a deep confidence come over me. I had never had someone anoint my head with oil while praying in tongues, but my strength was renewed, and I longboarded away, assured that God would continue to provide.

Even though I trusted God to supply places for me to sleep, my faith was really tested the day I left Fort Myers. I had only one confirmed host left in the entire state of Florida, and that was 130 miles (209 kilometers) away. From there, it would be another 700 miles (1,126 kilometers) to reach my next host in New Orleans. Given my daily average of 45 miles (72 kilometers), I anticipated numerous nights of uncertain accommodation. The reality of this began to sink in, casting doubt on my "no sleeping gear" decision. Seeking clarity, I found a quiet park by a small lake where I began explaining my doubts to God, starting with, *You really don't want me to take sleeping gear with me? How is this supposed to work?*

After some time, I pulled out of my backpack a small book called *Midnight Jesus* by Jamie Blaine; it was a gift from Kim Metzler. It's a collection of true-life stories of Jamie having divine encounters with everyday people looking for hope in their darkest hours. The stories resonated with me. I spent the entire day at the park enjoying Florida's mild January weather and this intriguing book. As dusk approached, I started wondering where I would rest for the night. Sometimes our faith is mixed with doubts, but it keeps moving forward. I knew I wasn't going to sleep in this park, so I jumped on my board and followed the road that led me over the Cape Coral bridge.

To calm my nerves, I decided to call my dear friend Grandma Anna, who lives in Pennsylvania. While she isn't my biological grandma, our bond is so strong that I affectionately call her my grandma. I would call her many times while out on the road. Our connection formed back when I was living in East Petersburg with Gammy and Pa. The way I met Grandma Anna can only be attributed to the Spirit of God. One Saturday morning, as I was praying and reading Scripture in my bedroom, that persistent, inner voice urged me, saying, *Step outside and talk to someone about Jesus.* Initially, I dismissed it because it sounded kind of weird. I didn't know anyone in the neighborhood, so why would I go talk to someone about Jesus? But I just couldn't shake the thought. Eventually, I stepped outside and wandered down the street, where I saw Grandma Anna walking her small white dog, Gracie, around the cul-de-sac.

"Nice day for a walk, huh?" I said as she and Gracie approached.

"Yes, it is," she replied just as we passed each other.

I thought about blurting out, *I'm on a mission to talk to someone about Jesus today*, but that felt too abrupt. Instead, I eased into the conversation with a simple question. "What's your dog's name?" That led to a five-minute conversation before I even mentioned Jesus. When I finally did, her face lit up, and she said, "Come, let me show you the Jesus I have!" Naturally, I followed and was introduced to a small stone statue of Jesus in her garden.

As we stood in her garden looking at Jesus, I tried to bring up more conversation, but I could sense her hesitation. She wasn't sure why a young guy like me would want to talk with a widow like her, but to me, I was just following the Shepherd's voice. I knew God had put her in my path for a reason, but I didn't realize why until three days later when I knocked on her door again. She opened the first door but stayed behind the screen, hesitating. Her eyes held a heaviness I hadn't seen before. For a moment, I wondered if she felt like I was intruding, but then she blurted out, "I have cancer, Daniel."

I didn't know what to say. The weight of it settled between us as I stood there, searching for words. Then her voice broke the silence. "Why is this happening?" she asked, her words filled with pain and confusion. I had no answer. All I could do was offer what I knew. "I'll pray for you," I said. And from that day forward, I did. Three months passed, and I hadn't heard from Anna. No returned calls, no answer at the door. I started to wonder if I had offended her. Maybe she didn't want me in her life anymore. But those were just my doubts speaking. Then, one day, a letter arrived in the mail from Anna. She explained to me with astonishment that the doctors had told her she was cancer-free! Later, she mentioned that while lying in the hospital during her treatments, she had wondered if I was an angel sent by God—our meeting had been that unexpected.

It crossed my mind that the cancer might return but now, nearly ten years later, she remains completely cancer-free. That one encounter turned into a deep friendship; Grandma Anna and I still talk to this day. I've spoken to her on the phone more than most other friends. Moments like this have taught me the importance of listening to that persistent, inner voice.

Back in Florida, the sun had just slipped below the rooftops, and I was still on my longboard, rolling down the dimly lit streets of Cape Coral while talking to Grandma Anna about the memories we'd made. Her voice was warm and steady, the kind that makes you feel like there is nothing to worry about, and then she asked, "So, where are you spending the night?" She always wanted to know that I was safe being out on my own and all.

I responded with, "I'm just trusting God to provide something tonight, but I don't know yet." That did nothing to reassure her, which I could feel from her small, worried pause on the phone. Then someone shouted from the parking lot I was skating through, "Hey, buddy!"

"I gotta go, Grandma Anna. I'll call you later," I said, eager to find out who was yelling at me. Much to my surprise, the person was calling to me from the front doors of the church whose parking lot I was riding through. As I approached, he asked me if I wanted to join their young adult group that evening. How fortuitous.

I attended the meeting and as the evening concluded, I hung around to help stack chairs and tidy up the room; this led me to make a connection with a friendly guy.

"What's your name?" he asked me.

"My name is Daniel. What's yours?"

"Jorge," he responded. "It's nice to meet you, Daniel. Are you from Cape Coral?"

"No, I'm actually from South Carolina."

"South Carolina, that's cool! What are you doing in Florida?"

"I'm traveling across America on a longboard."

After I said this, Jorge began to ask me a bunch more questions about my trip. He told me that he was inspired by my journey and faith. Then he started introducing me to all his friends by saying something like, "Bro, this guy is so rad! He's longboarding across the U.S. and came all the way from Miami already!" I greeted each of his friends with a smile and was genuinely interested in getting to know them. It turned out they had all planned to grab a late dinner at Chipotle Mexican Grill, and Jorge exclaimed, "Bro, you should totally join us!" Considering I had no other commitments, and I was hungry, I eagerly replied, "Absolutely!"

During our time together, I engaged more deeply with Jorge talking about God, faith, and my journey thus far. Then he asked me, "Where are you sleeping tonight?"

I responded, "Uh ... somewhere around here."

He raised his eyebrows and asked, "You're not sleeping outside, are you?"

When he found out that I didn't have any accommodations, he invited me to stay at his house for the night, if it was OK with his mom. I didn't want to impose, but the thought of sleeping outside with mosquitoes made me accept his kind offer. Then he called up his mom and spoke to her in Spanish. They were speaking so fast that, to me, it sounded like they were in a heated debate. I thought there was no way she was going to allow a stranger like me to sleep at their house. When he hung up, I figured I would be sleeping outside for sure. Then Jorge broke the news and said, "My mom said, 'Yes.'" I let out a deep breath and then leaned back in the passenger seat of Jorge's car as he began to drive home.

Jorge's house was huge and welcoming. His mother was in the middle of preparing an air mattress for me to sleep on in Jorge's room. It was a new experience for me to sleep in the house of a stranger I had known for only a couple hours, but I was so grateful. As his mom put the finishing touches on the accommodations, Jorge mentioned, "I need to go finish some homework for my classes tomorrow," and then left me sitting on his bed while his mom continued to make mine. Although her English wasn't the best, she expressed something along the lines of, "You are exactly the person my son needed to meet tonight. I see a divine presence within you." Tears welled up in her eyes, and she continued, "He has been searching intensely. It has been challenging, but tonight, I see a new light in his eyes because of you."

What does one say to a mother when she shares something like that? I thanked her for her hospitality and said how grateful I was to be able to be an inspiration to her son. When I lay in bed that night, all I thought was, *God is orchestrating something truly remarkable at this moment, and it's only the fourth night of a journey that may last for who knows how long.* I gazed at the ceiling, imagining how incredible this trip was going to be. It felt as though God was pleased with my faith and trust in His provision and actually listened to my requests. I thanked Him for a safe place to sleep, a splendid house, a comfy air mattress, and my new friend, Jorge.

The next morning, Jorge invited me to attend one of his college classes at Florida Gulf Coast University, and I gladly accepted. After class, we ate lunch at the cafeteria with his friends. Then he showed me around the campus and took pictures of me longboarding on the boardwalk next to Lakefront Beach. For dinner, we enjoyed Pub Subs sandwiches and watched the sunset over the palm trees on the horizon. Because I had no plans to stay with Jorge another night, I bid him farewell and continued my journey.

As darkness fell, the reality of not having a place to sleep returned. I longboarded for hours into the night on Highway 41. When I was too tired to go any further, I stopped in front of the Golf World Discount Shop and Driving Range in North Fort Myers. At 1:30 a.m., the parking lot was empty. Exhausted, I settled under the secluded pavilion next to the driving range. Using some cushions from nearby chairs, I made a bed on the concrete floor and lay down. Although it wasn't much, I was fairly comfortable, and I was grateful for another place to rest. I tried to stay alert, but I was so tired I quickly fell into a light sleep.

A few hours later, a car pulled up in the parking lot in front of the pavilion where I was sleeping, illuminating the area and waking me up. I didn't feel comfortable lying there anymore, so I put the cushions back, gathered my belongings, and made my way toward Highway 41. Having gotten only a few hours of sleep, I was dragging. As the sun came up, I cruised up to a Chick-fil-A where I grabbed breakfast and charged my phone. A married couple asked me about my board, and they were impressed when I told them about my journey. I wanted to engage with them more, but my mind was consumed by the pressing question of where I would sleep next. I hoped maybe this couple would generously offer me a place to stay, but that didn't happen.

After fueling up on food, I was back on the road, carving through the miles as the day stretched on. I went about five to eight miles an hour if the roads were good and would cover anywhere from twenty to eighty miles total depending on how I was feeling and the heat of the day. Often, I would stop at a gas station or Dollar General to get some food and water and then sit outside and rest for a while.

The pavement was mostly smooth that day, making for an easy ride, but every so often, cracks and uneven pavement sent vibrations up through my legs. I weaved between sidewalks and shoulders, dodging potholes and the occasional roadside debris. Strip malls, fast-food restaurants, and gas stations blurred past me, the lights from their signs flickered on as the sun began to set. At intersections, I had to stop and wait for the lights to change, the hum of traffic surrounding me. As nightfall descended, headlights cast long shadows on the pavement, and I stayed alert, scanning for safe spots to ride on.

I put on my headlamp to light the way, using it as much to guide me as to make sure I was seen. Skating at night had a completely different feel. For one, I was usually more tired, my thoughts hazy from the miles behind me. The roads were quieter, with fewer cars, but that also meant I was less visible, which always made me more cautious. The people out late at night were different too: some just getting off work, others out to have a good time, making me more aware of my surroundings. The silence was heavier, the air cooler, and the world felt a little lonelier. I kept pushing forward until I no longer needed my headlamp, rolling into the glow of a brightly lit Wal-Mart parking lot.

It was already past midnight, and I thought I might find a place to lie down for a few hours. I walked behind the massive blue supercenter and discovered a fenced-in area with a small gate that was unlocked. Inside were big pallets stacked with folded cardboard boxes. I climbed on top of one that was chest high and lay down because I figured it would be better than sleeping on the ground. Lying on the pile of trash, I asked God, *Do You really want me to journey across America like this, sleeping outside in weird places? What if I got a tent? Wal-Mart sells them, you know.* Suddenly, I remembered a few years ago a buddy from college told me about an app where people would host you in their homes for free, but I couldn't recall the app's name. *God, what's it called?* I asked. After a few moments, it suddenly came to me—the Couchsurfing app.

Anticipation surged in me as I downloaded the app and created an account. I found a host available in Sarasota, Florida, just thirty miles north of my location. I crafted a message requesting a two-night stay, hoping for a day off between longboarding sessions. I wanted to ask if I could stay longer but didn't want to impose. With my message sent, I lay back down on my cardboard bed and drifted into slumber beneath the twinkling stars.

The next morning, I woke up to a Wal-Mart employee throwing more cardboard in through the gate. I quickly hid behind a pallet and waited for them to leave. Then I looked at my phone and noticed a response from the host in Sarasota. To my delight, a notification appeared, "Tom has accepted your request for two nights." Excitement and relief filled me at the same time. I quickly thanked this new host and inquired about his address.

After a long and hot thirty miles, I arrived at a very well-kept trailer park in the late afternoon. Tom lived in a retirement community of nice trailer homes only a mile from the beautiful sandy shore of Siesta Key Beach. When I approached on my board, Tom came out to welcome me. "You must be Daniel," he said, shaking my hand. "Welcome to my humble abode. It's good to see you. Come in." His welcoming demeanor put me at ease.

It turned out Tom had been a host on the app for a while, but I was only his second guest. He had a room prepared for me, and I even had my own bathroom. Although I knew the app said that the accommodation was free, it felt hard to believe, so I asked, "How much do I owe you for this?"

"It's free!" Tom replied. "You shouldn't pay anyone money on this app. It's a way to meet travelers, make new friends, and hear their stories. Sometimes guests will bring a small gift or something, but you shouldn't ever pay anything. You can pay it forward by hosting people in your home someday."

Tom was such a nice guy that he even offered me dinner. Over dinner, Tom told me he was seventy-two years old and had a son and sister he didn't see much. He didn't go into details, but I could tell it caused him some pain. Tom had a PhD in law from the University of Oxford and a master's degree from Georgetown University in Washington, DC, which he mentioned was founded by Jesuits. He further shared that he had previously worked as a private tutor for the children of a wealthy European family. And at some point, he even taught as a university professor. Intrigued by all his accomplishments, I continued asking him questions about his life. Eventually, I circled back around to his comment about the Jesuits and asked what it meant to be a Jesuit. Well, this question began the conversation of Tom's spiritual journey.

After dinner, we sat on his back porch, and Tom asked me about my spiritual journey. I told him I grew up a preacher's kid, went to Bible university, and followed Jesus. When I finished, he leaned back and said, "Well, now that I know you're a Christian, I feel compelled to share something personal with you."

"Go for it," I said.

"I'm … gay," he answered, his voice carried a small hesitation, as if he were holding his breath, waiting to see what would happen next. He had a son, so I guessed this was something he had come to terms with later in life, maybe not long ago. Caught off guard, I said, "Thanks for telling me, Tom. I really appreciate you sharing that. I think you are a great person, and I hope we can build a real friendship. I am attracted to women, but that does not have to stop us from being friends. I am glad to be here, and I am grateful you trusted me with something so personal."

A slow, genuine smile spread across his face like someone letting out a held breath. He leaned forward and said, "I have never acted on it. I just do not feel attraction toward women; that is how I recognize my sexuality." He paused and then asked me a question, "What do you think, Daniel? Since you are a Christian, do you think it is wrong?"

Tom's question made me a little nervous because I did not want to introduce tension into a friendship that was just starting, but it did not stop me from engaging. These conversations can be awkward, but I believe they are necessary, the kind that make you want to swallow something down your throat, even though there's nothing there. But rather than tossing out a quick answer, I decided to ask a question back. "Before I tell you my thoughts, Tom, is there any form of sexuality that you condemn?"

He paused for a moment and looked up, as if he was searching for his answer. "No, I don't think I would. Love is love, and everyone should be able to choose whoever they want to love."

"What about a mother and son who want to love each other?" I asked. "What about adults who want to 'love' animals or even children? It's kind of uncomfortable to talk about these things, but they are real issues we need to consider. Sex is a powerful act. It can be a means of deepening a physical and spiritual bond between a committed couple, or it can be used as a weapon, a form of violence against one's soul. 'Love is love' sounds great, but it does absolutely nothing for us intellectually. It's a circular definition that leaves us just as ignorant as we were before. Imagine opening a dictionary, and on the first page it's written: 'Aardvark means aardvark.' What if the rest of the dictionary continued to define everything in the same fashion? I would advise you to throw that dictionary away. We should do the same with this deeply flawed phrase 'love is love.'"

Tom abruptly cut in, "Well, hold on there, Daniel. The statement 'love is love' doesn't apply to animals or children because they cannot consent."

"I see your point," I responded, "but there is one major flaw to this line of reasoning. Adults make children do many things they do not consent to doing, like eating their vegetables, tying their shoes, attending school, and going to bed at a certain time. The argument that children cannot consent can be easily reasoned away, leaving them vulnerable. Obviously, we both agree that we should draw some boundaries around children, but this reveals that you do condemn some form of sexuality, Tom. So, since we both believe in boundaries, the question is, whose boundaries should we follow and why?"

"I'm tracking with you," Tom said. "So where do you draw the line, Daniel?" he asked.

"I'll admit, I don't hold a popular position within our society. I believe that sex should be reserved for a life-long, committed monogamous heterosexual adult relationship because this is where our Creator has drawn the line. Now, I don't know if you believe in the existence of God or not, but I do. And I believe in the words He spoke to us revealed through the Scriptures which say, 'Therefore a man shall leave his father and mother and be joined to his wife, and they shall become one flesh,' (Genesis 2:24). In short, one man and one woman for life. Anything else is immoral according to God's standard.

I believe this is the strongest foundation for sexual guidelines because it isn't based on any human reasoning or opinion; it's based on the Word of God. Now, whether you believe in His words or not is another matter, but that is my answer. What do you think?" I asked Tom this question because I am convinced that, as Christians, we must give our answer with gentleness and respect to anyone with a differing belief (1 Peter 3:15).

Tom and I continued to go back and forth calmly and respectfully, but at the end of our conversation, we still didn't agree. I told Tom, "If we had to agree with every friend about everything, we would have no friends. I want to be your friend because I believe you're a great guy. I mean, you're a complete stranger hosting me in your house for two nights. Not many people would do something like that, and I admire you for it."

Tom smiled and said, "Of course we can still be friends. And you know what, Daniel? I really like you, and I've definitely enjoyed this conversation. I hope to have more quality conversations like this for as long as you stay here. I want you to know that you're welcome to stay at my house for as long as you want."

When he expressed this, I lit up with a big smile saying, "That really means a lot to me, Tom! Thank you. I guess I'll let you know tomorrow how long I'd like to stay."

The sun had already set, and it was getting late, so we both decided to head to our rooms.

"Good night, Daniel!"

"Good night, Tom. Sleep well," I said as I walked toward the guest room. When I climbed into the soft bed, I was glad to be warm, glad to be inside again, and glad to have met Tom.

The next morning, I took a shower in the guest bathroom, where Tom had thoughtfully placed a towel and all the toiletries I needed. Feeling refreshed, I walked into the kitchen for breakfast, and Tom offered me some oatmeal packs. "Help yourself," he said. I took two strawberry-flavored packs and heated them in the microwave while he finished up his own meal. As we ate, I told him, "I'd like to stay for a week if that's alright with you. Being on the road and sleeping outside the past couple nights has really worn me out."

He smiled and nodded. "Of course, stay as long as you need." His generosity was humbling, and I knew I wanted to do something to give back.

After finishing my meal, I decided to longboard to the store to pick up some groceries. The ride was easy, the sun warm, and the breeze coming off the coast made it a perfect day to longboard. While walking the aisles of the store, a thought popped into my mind: *Why don't you make dinner for Tom every night you stay at his house?* It felt like a simple but meaningful way to show gratitude, and I figured the thought must be from God. So, I grabbed enough groceries for the two of us and headed back to Tom's house.

Longboarding back from the store with groceries wasn't too difficult. After spending so much time on my board, it was starting to feel a part of me. I put the heavy items in my backpack and carried two plastic bags in each hand, careful to keep my balance. When I walked in the front door of Tom's house and told him that I was making dinner for us, he seemed a little surprised but didn't protest. He just nodded and said, "Alright, let's see what you got." I had learned a thing or two about cooking from my mom, but most of what I knew came from trial and error. That night, I made a creamy chicken pasta with bowtie noodles, sautéed onions, diced tomatoes, and a rich, cheesy sauce. The smell of garlic and butter filled the kitchen as everything came together.

Tom set out some cranberry juice for us while I finished up. When I brought the skillet to the table, our bowls sat empty, ready to be filled. Before we started eating, I snapped a quick picture to capture the moment. In the photo, I'm grinning and throwing up a Shaka sign, while Tom sits across from me with a calm, content expression. The kitchen around us felt homey. It was a well-used space with warm wooden cabinets and simple decor that gave off a welcoming, lived-in vibe. It wasn't just a meal; it was a moment of connection, and I wanted to remember it.

Then I asked if I could bless the food. "Go ahead," Tom said with a nod. I offered a simple prayer, thanking God for the meal and the company, then served up our food. After the first couple of bites, Tom spoke up. "Not bad," he mumbled with pasta still in his mouth. We ate slowly, talking about life, travel, and the little things that make a place feel like home. It was a simple meal, but it carried more weight than just eating food. It was a moment of connection, of gratitude, and of sharing life, even if just for a short time.

Tom truly appreciated my company during my stay, and most evenings, we would unwind in the community pool and hot tub, gazing up at the stars. It was a week of pure relaxation, something I hadn't experienced in a while. With the extra downtime, I caught up on journaling and made a few phone calls. One morning, I called Trevor Heinrich, a friend from Lancaster County, Pennsylvania. He was someone I looked up to, not just because of his contagious smile and charismatic personality but because of his adventurous spirit; he had walked across America back in 2013. Before I started my own journey, Trevor had given me his neon green safety vest, the same one he had worn while crossing the country. Now, as I skated my way west, I carried that piece of his journey with me across America again.

As I was on the phone with him that morning, we spent three hours swapping stories, talking about our travel adventures, and praying together. I told Trevor about the conversation I had with Tom, and he told me, "While I was out on the road, I met all different kinds of people. My purpose was to bring the love of Jesus to those who needed hope." His words stuck and encouraged me to bring the love of Jesus to *everyone* along the way.

Throughout the week, I experienced the kindheartedness of Tom in a way I hadn't expected. On my third morning at his house, he laid out a couple of extra pieces of clothing for me, knowing I only had three shirts, two pairs of shorts, and a pair of pants. It was a small gesture, but it spoke volumes. As we spent more time together, I got to know him beyond just being a generous host. He shared parts of his life, including the loneliness he often felt. He told me his sister lived nearby, but she didn't visit anymore. He thought it might have had something to do with the way he expressed his sexuality. I didn't know what to say, but I appreciated that Tom trusted me enough to share about his personal life. Sometimes, the road introduced me to people who just needed someone to listen to them. And for those seven days, I was grateful to be that person for Tom.

Toward the end of the week, Tom treated me to dinner a couple of times, taking me to two of his favorite spots, including a local seafood place he loved. We sat on the patio and reminisced over the fun we had enjoyed the past few days; one experience was we had watched most of Tom's favorite movies and TV series. When Sunday morning came around, I mentioned that a friend on Instagram had recommended a church in the area to attend. It was called South Shore Community Church. I asked Tom if he wanted to come with me, and he said yes.

We hopped into his small red car, drove to the church, and were greeted warmly upon arrival. In the auditorium, we sang songs and listened to the pastor's message. Afterward, Tom complimented the quality of the pastor's sermon, which meant a lot coming from a seasoned teacher like him. Then Tom told me that he was going to track down the pastor and express his appreciation. While waiting for Tom, I struck up a conversation with a friendly guy named Jacob, who later joined us for lunch at a cozy restaurant called Word of Mouth.

After returning to Tom's house, I began packing my belongings, knowing I had to leave the next morning. Tom repeatedly urged me to extend my stay, but as much as I enjoyed Tom's company, I knew I had to continue my journey. That evening, we watched the Philadelphia Eagles beat the New England Patriots in Super Bowl LII. It felt like a good way to end my time at Tom's house.

When morning arrived and I was ready to go, Tom went over to his kitchen drawer, grabbed a spare key, and told me, "You always have a place here, Daniel; you can return anytime." Then he placed the key in my hand and said, "I've genuinely enjoyed hosting you, and I wish you the best on your journey." I felt deeply honored and accepted the key, which I've kept in my backpack ever since as a memento of the cherished moments I spent with Tom. It was hard to walk out his front door and leave, but I had to keep going. I set my board on the ground and rolled down his driveway waving goodbye. Tom stood on his porch waving back as I disappeared around the corner.

In the weeks that followed, I maintained regular contact with Tom as I cruised down the roads of America on my longboard. During one of our phone conversations, he shared some exciting news. "I'm still attending that church, Daniel."

"Really?" I exclaimed.

"Yes. I've made more friends now, and the pastor knows me too. I even participate in a small group each week."

"That's fantastic, Tom! I'm thrilled to hear you're making new friends," I replied.

"Me too!" Tom said. "And when people ask how I found this church, I tell them, 'A friendly guy on a longboard came to my house and then brought me here.'"

We both chuckled, and then Tom added, "I want to start serving in this church too."

I was a little surprised but excited to hear that Tom had found a welcoming community and was eager to serve others. Then he confided in me, saying, "Daniel, I believe that Jesus is making a real and meaningful impact in my life. I'm feeling more optimistic and hopeful these days. And something else is gradually changing—I'm starting to find women more attractive. It's not that I'm interested in anyone, but I'm noticing them again." My face light up as I glided down the road on my longboard. I was glad to hear that the love of Jesus had reached my friend Tom exactly where he was at.

A few months later, an email from Tom arrived, notifying me of his new phone number, so I decided to give him a call. "Hello, this is Tom," he answered.

"Tom! What's up, my friend? It's Daniel!" I exclaimed.

"Daniel, it's so good to hear your voice!"

"It's good to hear yours too, Tom. How are you?" I inquired.

He replied slowly, "Well, I'm not at my house anymore."

"Why, what happened?" I asked with curiosity.

Tom paused for a second and took a breath as he prepared to explain. "A few weeks ago, I was walking down my driveway to fetch the mail. Just a simple thing, you know, something I've done a thousand times. But my foot caught a crack in the pavement, and I went down hard. The pain was sharp, like a knife in my neck. I couldn't move. I just laid there helpless. My neighbor noticed me sprawled out on the pavement. They called the ambulance, which took me to the hospital. The doctors ran X-rays and told me I'd broken a vertebra in my neck." Tom paused, his breath uneven, as if the memory still stung a bit. "I'm in a nursing home now, Daniel. That's why I have a new phone number. It's hard to say but…" His voice cracked, barely above a whisper. "None of my family has visited."

The words landed like a stone in my chest, sinking deep. I pictured Tom, my friendly host, now frail in a sterile room, waiting for a familiar face that never came. My throat tightened, and I didn't know how to respond; the silence between us was thick and sad. But then Tom's voice lifted, soft but steady. "There is good news, though, Daniel. Most of the time, I don't have time to think about it."

I listened closer, desperate for some hope. "How's that, Tom?" I asked.

His words came slowly, each one wrapped in grateful wonder, as if he could hardly believe what had happened. "The church you introduced me to … some folks from there have been visiting me. They sit by my bed, talk about the weather, share stories, laugh with me. It's like they've filled up the holes. Their kindness is keeping me afloat. And I need you to know…" His voice wavered, as if he had been carrying this gratitude in silence until now, "It's because of you."

My eyes burned as his words settled into me. I saw him in that nursing home bed, surrounded by strangers who'd become family; their presence was a small miracle born from a single connection I'd made. My eye couldn't hold back the warm tears spilling over my eyelids and rolling down my cheeks from awe at how God had used me. My voice broke as I said, "I love you, Tom." The words felt small against the fullness in my heart, but they were all I had to offer through the phone that tied us together across the miles. This moment had a significant impact on my life—one I will never forget.

I want to share with you now the review Tom left me on the Couchsurfing app in February of 2018 from Sarasota, Florida:

Daniel and I found we had much in common beginning with sharing. He is educated and knowledgeable and most willing to sit and talk. He also makes good apple bread and chocolate chip cookies. :-) He is a gentleman who can accommodate himself to any home and people. I actually will miss him when he needs to leave. He is most welcome to my home at any time. Even gave him a key to the house.

Over the years, I've often reflected back on that moment when my friend said, "Bro, you're longboarding across America;

you have to bring a tent!" By all practical logic, I should have set out with the usual camping gear. Yet that still, small voice continued whispering to me, *What if you put your trust in God to provide for your needs along the way?* It challenged the notion that following a whim would be reckless. But if I had ignored God's leading to forgo camping gear, I would have missed out on some amazing relationships. So, the next time you feel the small, persistent, inner voice guiding you somewhere unusual or even nudging you to do the illogical, don't brush it off. Test it. It might just be God's strategy to bring about divine encounters and moments of eternal impact.

CHAPTER 4.

BREAD FROM HEAVEN

FEBRUARY 5 – 22, 2018

SARASOTA TO LIVE OAK, FLORIDA

I used to imagine that God's miraculous provision was something reserved for Bible stories, but now I believe that God still provides in mysterious ways.

I wasn't able to leave Tom's house until 10:30 a.m. that Monday morning, since I had to wait for the rain to pass. My next host was on the north side of Tampa, Florida, about seventy miles away. His name was Victor. I had a long day ahead of me, but the weather delay turned out to be a blessing, cooling the air and making for a pleasant ride. Along the way, I found a wild orange tree, and the fresh citrus made for a perfect snack.

As the day stretched on, my phone battery drained until it finally died, leaving me without navigation or a way to contact Victor. I prayed, *God, help me find a place to charge my phone.* A few minutes later, I spotted exactly what I needed: an outdoor outlet on the side of a gas station, with a bench right next to it. I plugged in my phone and sat down, letting the exhaustion of the day settle in while I waited for enough charge to power it back on.

When my phone finally turned on, I saw a message from Victor. He had been checking in, asking where I was and how far I had left to go. I called him back and let him know my location. That's when he told me he had decided to come a bit south that evening to visit some friends, which put him much closer to me than we had originally planned. Instead of having to push my longboard several more miles to his house, I only had to go a short distance to make it to his friend's apartment.

When I arrived, Victor and his friends welcomed me in like family. Dinner was already prepared, and after a long day on the road, I was beyond grateful to sit down and share a meal with people my age. We spent some time talking and relaxing before heading back to Victor's place in his car.

When we arrived, he mentioned that he lived with his mom and sister, and I had the opportunity to meet them in the kitchen. They were warm, welcoming, and immediately made me feel at home. In Victor's bedroom, I saw that he had already set up a small inflatable mattress for me across from his bed. It was a simple but thoughtful gesture, and I appreciated the effort. I didn't stay up long—after journaling, brushing my teeth, and taking out my contacts, I crawled into bed, grateful for the kindness I had received.

"Good night, Victor," I said, as I pulled the bed sheets over my shoulder.

"Good night, Dan," he replied as he switched off the light. Within minutes, we were both out.

The next morning was February 6, and the sun was beaming bright through the window. Neither of us slept in, since we both had things to do. I had made it a habit to start each day by reading a portion of the Bible, slowly working my way through it with the goal of finishing it during my trip.

The practice helped me stay grounded and consistent. As I pulled out my leather Bible, Victor looked over and asked, "What book is that?"

"It's actually a bunch of books that have been collected over the course of history, stories that lead to Jesus," I answered.

"So, it's the Bible," Victor said.

"Yeah," I said with a smile. "You're right. I just try not to use that word too often. It can start to feel distant or overly religious. Thinking of it as a collection of books helps me remember it's made up of real stories from real people. I used to think those stories were just for people long ago, but I've come to see that God still works in similar ways today."

Victor nodded. "Yeah, my mom is a Mormon, so I know about the Bible. Anyways, you want some breakfast?"

I couldn't say no to that. Victor whipped up some breakfast burritos with sausage and eggs and then pulled out something unfamiliar to me.

"You ever had Turkish coffee?" he asked, holding up a little copper pot.

"Nope," I said.

He smiled. "Oh man, you're in for a treat. It's strong and will wake you right up."

He explained how it was made: finely ground coffee beans simmered slowly in water with just a bit of sugar, never stirred once it started boiling. It was thick, bold, and came in a small cup. I took a sip and nearly coughed. "That's got a kick," I said, blinking a few times.

Victor laughed. "Dude, I told you! It's strong stuff. It's not your average coffee. It's like a wake-up call in a cup."

Victor and I enjoyed breakfast together, then I packed up my things. He drove me back to the spot where I had left off, and we said our goodbyes. It was so nice to meet another great Couchsurfer. I expressed my gratitude to Victor for his hospitality, gave him a hug, and set off on my longboard. My next stop was Hudson, Florida, where I'd be meeting up with Kim Metzler from Lancaster Bible College. A few days earlier, she had messaged me out of the blue:

> *Hi Dan, I'm keeping you in my thoughts and prayers during your longboarding trip. I noticed on Facebook that you're in southern*

Florida. I'll be at Word of Life Bible Institute north of Tampa this week doing an admissions presentation for LBC. Not sure how close you are to Hudson, but if you're nearby, it'd be great to catch up. Their campus can accommodate you, and your alumni status could help us with our LBC presentation. Let me know your thoughts.

Word of Life Bible Institute is a one-or two-year program where students live in community, study the Bible deeply, and grow in their faith. High school graduates often use it as a gap year before continuing their education or entering ministry. Kim's role was to connect with students finishing their time at Word of Life and encourage them to consider continuing their education at LBC with an associate or bachelor's degree. I let her know I was on my way and planned to meet her at the WOL campus that evening. From where I was, I had about thirty-five miles to cover.

A couple of hours into my journey, I was headed north on a smooth bike path called the Suncoast Trail; it runs alongside the Suncoast Parkway through the counties of Hillsborough, Pasco, Hernando, and Citrus. Longboarding on well-maintained pavement was a true pleasure, offering comfort and allowing me to cruise at top speed, about ten miles per hour. This meant that with a few breaks, I could reach Kim in about four and a half hours.

It was a radiant Tuesday afternoon, with the sun casting its warm glow through the dense woodlands on my left and the parkway on my right. From time to time, I'd pass by fellow cyclists or joggers who were also enjoying the beautiful day. In the distance, I noticed a small pavilion coming up on the right side of the trail. Under its roof was a picnic table that had a large orange drink dispenser sitting on top of it. *Oh, God, please let there be water in that cooler,* I prayed in my mind. To my delight, the cooler was full, so I filled my water bottle to the top. As I sat down on the picnic table to enjoy a brief respite, a bicyclist whizzed by going the same direction I had been traveling. Suddenly, he stopped and turned around; I figured he must have seen the orange cooler and decided to come back for a drink. When he approached the pavilion, he said, "Hey, are you that guy who is longboarding across America?"

I was shocked! He didn't look familiar, so I was completely baffled that he knew who I was. "Yes, I am," I admitted with a surprised tone in my voice.

"I knew it!" he shouted. "I can't believe it's you!"

I smiled in response to his excitement. "How did you know that?" I asked.

"Someone shared a Facebook post about a dude longboarding across America. I think I saw a picture of you on the beach in Miami. I can't believe I'm seeing you in person!" he said.

I couldn't believe that someone recognized me from a Facebook post. His name was John, and I found out that John was a pretty remarkable guy himself. He had done a few tours across the U.S. with his bicycle. His most recent one was from Florida to Oregon. His life had completely changed after quitting his 9-to-5 job and hitting the open road with his bike. We shared stories for almost an hour, even though it felt like ten minutes. I was so inspired by his stories and his positive attitude.

"You know," he told me, "after I left my job, sometimes I would see my old friends who I used to work with. They would tell me, 'John, your stories and all your experiences are incredible. I'm sure jealous of all the fun you're having.' But the thing is, Dan," John told me, "none of them would actually do anything to bring some change into their life. They would just keep working the same office job day after day, expecting a cool experience to just be delivered at their front door by UPS or something. Well, we both know that's never gonna happen, so I'd tell them, 'You gotta get yourself out there and start living before you die because life's too short, and you can't buy this stuff on Amazon!"

This short time with John fueled my passion for adventure. "Until next time, Brother!" John said as he jumped on his bicycle.

"See ya later, Bro!" I called out as he took off. He traveled twice my speed, so I watched John become a small speck in the distance until I couldn't see him anymore. I haven't seen him since that day, but his words still ring true. The experiences you have on the open road can't be delivered by Amazon. Don't wait for an incredible moment to show up at your front door. There's no guarantee it's coming. Life's too short, and it's up to you to make the most of it.

Meeting a new person exuding good energy from their spirit was refreshing. I had a big smile on my face and felt full of life as I continued cruising down the trail, and that's just about the time that my cell phone began to ring. It was Kim Metzler.

"Hey, Kim."

"Dan! Where are you at right now?" Kim quickly asked.

"Umm … I'm headed north somewhere on the Suncoast Trial following Highway 589. Maybe an hour away from Hudson. Why, what's up?"

I could tell that Kim was excited about something. "Are you feeling spontaneous?" she asked.

I grinned. "Yah! What is it?"

"Well, there's this heavy metal band called August Burns Red performing at The Ritz Ybor in Tampa Bay tonight. I'm not really into heavy metal, but I know the lead drummer, Matthew Greiner. I used to babysit him when he was a kid. I saw that he was performing in the city tonight, so I just called him up and asked if he would like to go to dinner before his show. He said yes! Then I asked if I could bring you and my colleague along, and he said that it'd be fine. So, we are headed south on the Suncoast Parkway right now and can pick you up on the side of the highway. Whaddya say?"

"Heck yeah! I'm totally down for that!" I exclaimed.

About ten minutes later, a car pulled over to the side of the road. It was Kim and her colleague, Emily, who I had known from my college days. I clambered over the fence separating the bike trail from the highway and gave Kim a hug before hopping into their rental car.

"Dan! It's fantastic to see you!" Kim exclaimed. I sat in the back seat as she began to head toward Tampa. Seeing familiar faces brought a sense of comfort. As we drove, I shared with Kim and Emily about staying with Tom and Jorge and my recent encounter with John, who had recognized me from the social media post. She was thrilled to hear that my story was gaining exposure and inspiring others.

We parked and walked toward the rear entrance of the venue in the historic Ybor City entertainment district of Tampa. Kim spotted Matt in the distance just as he was heading our way. His athletic build and clean-cut, casual style carried a steady, grounded presence that caught my eye before he even spoke. He was nothing like the heavy metal drummer you'd picture. "Kim!" he called out with a big smile as they embraced warmly. "It's so good to see you."

Soon, Kim introduced Emily and me to the renowned drummer of August Burns Red. Despite his fame, Matt greeted us warmly, shaking our hands, looking us in the eye, and making us feel welcomed. There was nothing flashy or self-important about him, as he seemed humble and kind.

While Kim and Matt talked and caught up, we strolled down the street to a nearby restaurant called James Joyce Irish Pub & Eatery and met up with one of Matt's friends, Tal, and his girlfriend. We found a cozy table and settled in for a laid-back meal and some light conversation. Matt spent most of the time reconnecting with Kim and Tal, but at one point, he looked over at me and asked, "You longboarded all the way from where?"

"Miami," I said.

He nodded with a grin. "That's wild, man."

That was about the extent of our conversation, but I enjoyed listening as they shared stories. Tal's girlfriend asked me more about my trip, and we ended up chatting while the others talked. When it was time to pay, Kim generously paid for my delicious burger, which was exactly what I needed after a long day on the board.

Following dinner, we made our way back to the venue. Before heading inside, I snapped a quick photo with Matt and Tal in front of the building, a moment I wanted to remember. I already felt like I had met some incredible people on this journey, and I hadn't even left Florida yet.

Matt walked us over to the ticket booth and generously provided each of us with passes to the show. Then he invited us to hang out on the tour bus while the band got ready. Inside, the rest of the band was relaxing before their performance; the atmosphere was calm but expectant. Matt introduced us to each of them, and we spent some time chatting while sitting on the plush leather couches, soaking in the rare glimpse behind the scenes.

Eventually, the band headed backstage, and we made our way into the venue to find our seats. Although heavy metal wasn't normally my genre, the energy in the room was electric. Lights pulsed, the crowd surged, and the music hit like a wave. I even jumped into the mosh pit at the center of the auditorium for a few wild minutes before watching Matt deliver an unforgettable drum solo. The whole experience was intense, completely different from anything I had expected, and thrilling from start to finish.

It was hard to believe where I was and how it had all unfolded. It felt like a dream, yet the whole encounter was so tangible and real. It was the perfect culmination of events to reinforce everything John shared with me on the trail. Florida became a magnet for the unexpected; it seemed to bring me face to face with increasingly exciting experiences. The further north I ventured, the more familiar I became with the unpredictable.

After the concert, Kim drove me back to Word of Life Bible Institute, where I stayed for a few nights and helped with an LBC admissions presentation by sharing about my own college experience there. The next morning, Kim dropped me off at the same spot on the Suncoast Trail where she had picked me up. I longboarded back to campus, stayed one more night in a student cabin, and spent the day journaling, meeting students, and relaxing by the pool.

After Hudson, I continued north to Wildwood, where I stayed with a Couchsurfing host named Terry, who had over 500 glowing reviews. From there, I pushed on to Gainesville and stayed with another host named Kiernan, a University of Florida alumnus. He let me borrow his bike to explore the city, and after a short conversation with two women I randomly met at a baseball game, one of them surprised me the next day with a packed lunch at the library where I was spending most of my time reading and relaxing. It was a small gesture, but it reminded me how much kindness I encountered along the way. Even during the slower moments, the journey was still full of adventures and unexpected provision.

I spent a lot of time searching for my next Couchsurfing host, but options were limited on my route north. The only person listed within longboarding distance was a man named Bruce. So, I sent him a request and waited. Later that afternoon, his reply came in: "I am currently in Australia."

Disappointed but understanding, I responded, "No worries! Have a great time!" I didn't want to overstay my welcome with Kiernan, but I wasn't sure what else to do. So, I prayed, trusting that God would provide a place. Not long after, another message from Bruce lit up my phone. "If you can't find a place," he wrote, "let me know, and I can give you the code to the lockbox. The house is empty. You can crash there and use the bed and shower."

I sat there stunned. A man I had never met, currently on the other side of the world, had just offered me his home. His simple kindness felt like an answer straight from heaven. I was reminded once again that God sees, God hears, and often His provision shows up through the generosity of a stranger.

I left Kiernan's house early on Monday morning. The bright sun beamed down over my head as I cruised along, but the February temperature was relatively mild. With the smooth pavement and flat terrain stretching for miles, longboarding was considerably more pleasant. I would set small goals for myself to keep my mind stimulated, aiming for the next mile marker on the road or the next patch of shade beneath the extended branches of a tree. These tactics would help my mind stay focused on continuing as I also listened to upbeat music and thought-provoking podcasts.

I had the highway mostly to myself. Civilization was hours away, and I hadn't seen a single car in quite some time. I could feel the vibrations of my rubber wheels gently rumbling over the asphalt as my longboard glided down the road. I wasn't going very fast. Then the wind picked up and blew across the field next to me; the tall golden reed grass swayed in wind like waves on the ocean rolling over the water. Suddenly, I felt very alone.

Off in the distance, beyond the field, a small one-story house emerged beneath the shade of a towering oak tree whose leaves gracefully danced in the wind. The house appeared recently abandoned, yet it exuded a welcoming spirit. I put my foot down, paused my music, and took out my earbuds. The world became quiet as the wind caressed my face. All of a sudden, I was overwhelmed by an inexplicable wave of emotion. I didn't quite comprehend it at the time, but in retrospect, I believe it was the tangible presence of God's

Spirit surrounding me. This was a very unique experience for me, and I still wasn't sure what exactly I was feeling.

Then it was as if my spirit deeply desired to communicate or pray something to God, yet I lacked the words to express my feelings. I began to let out utterances that I didn't understand with my mind, yet it felt like my spirit was actually saying something I couldn't communicate with my own words. I had never done anything like that before, although I had read about it in the New Testament, specifically in the first letter to the Corinthians, chapter fourteen. It felt compelling and genuine, also a bit strange and out of this world. The whole thing lasted twenty or thirty seconds, and I had full control of myself the entire time. Once I finished speaking, I sensed that I had just said something significant to God in the Spirit. "What did I just pray?" I asked under my breath. Immediately, I felt a response from God in my heart: *You just asked for Bible stories to happen in your life*. I knew the thought must have been from God because it was so random. Plus, it seemed like a good request, so I just believed it and anticipated the outcome. I got back on my board and pushed myself down the rolling closer and closer to Live Oak.

Longboarding to the address Bruce provided, I found a charming one-story brick house nestled in a serene neighborhood. Despite the stellar reviews on his profile, a hint of doubt lingered in my mind. Never had a stranger extended such hospitality to me. Would I discover the promised lockbox, and would the code actually work?

Approaching the side door, I was startled by a noise around the corner. An older man with a paintbrush in his hand walked out from behind the back of the house. "Who are you?" he asked.

Caught off guard, I nervously replied, "I'm Daniel. Is this Bruce's house?" I wondered if I had walked up to the wrong one because I hadn't expected anyone to be home.

The man eyed me with curiosity and said, "Yes, is he expecting you? He's in Australia right now, you know."

Feeling uneasy, I explained, "Bruce gave me the code to his lockbox and told me I could stay here. Is that OK?"

"Well," he responded, "if Bruce said you could stay, then it's all good. My name's David, by the way."

It was around 5 p.m. by then, and David was just starting to gather his paint supplies to go home for the night. We engaged in light conversation, and he explained that he had been painting the back side of Bruce's house. Eventually, he bid me farewell and drove off.

The lockbox was right where Bruce said it would be. I entered the code, and to my amazement, the lockbox opened, and the key was inside. It was so surreal, pushing open the door of the empty house of a complete stranger who was halfway around the world. Everything aligned with Bruce's description. I found a nice bed and shower just like he said. I was overwhelmed with gratitude as I remembered, only a couple weeks ago, I was sleeping outside on some cardboard boxes behind a Wal-Mart. It was an unexpected blessing that taught me a lot about hospitality.

The next morning, I skated to Subway for brunch. Bringing my leather-bound Bible along, I took a seat at a table and delved into the next chapter in my reading. I was on a journey through the entire Bible and found myself at the end of 1 Kings and into the beginning of 2 Kings, which recounts the stories of Elijah's life. I read about the drought that had swept over the land of Israel when God led Elijah to a small brook, where ravens dropped him bread and meat in the morning and evening while he drank water from the brook. *Wouldn't it be nice, God, if You sent a bird to bring me some food while I'm out longboarding?* I prayed to myself. *Perhaps a Subway sandwich or something.* I imagined a raven gracefully swooping in, carrying a sandwich, and echoing a resounding, "Ca-caw," before dropping it into my hands and soaring away. *Wishful thinking,* I thought with a smile.

The following day, Wednesday, February 21, I was sitting outside the Live Oak library, where I had spent most of the day utilizing the wi-fi. With the library closing at 5 p.m., I relocated outside and settled on a wooden bench overlooking the nearly deserted parking lot as the sun began to gradually dip below the horizon and paint beautiful streaks of color in the sky. I decided to call my friend John Zliczewski from back home; he was someone I often called during my trip. While talking with John, I witnessed something so wild.

"Bro!" I said interrupting our conversation.

"What?" John asked.

"You won't believe this, Bro!"

"What?!" he responded eagerly.

"A bird just flew right in front of me and dropped a piece of bread!" I exclaimed in total amazement.

"No way, dude!" John said.

Rushing over to the wonder bread, I told him, "I was reading about this in the Bible yesterday, and now it just happened! Am I dreaming right now? This can't be! Have you ever seen a bird drop bread right in front of somebody? And the bird was black and was probably a raven, just like the Bible story!"

"That's mad wild, Bro," John said. And then, with a touch of humor, he suggested, "You should eat it. Maybe you'll become a prophet!"

We both burst out laughing. "I guess I have to eat it," I said, "but first I gotta show this to someone because this is unreal." To capture the moment, I took a picture of the bread and sent it to John. Then I picked it up, and neither of us could believe what had just happened. "It's Wednesday night," I said. "There's probably some church having a midweek service. Maybe I could encourage some people with the story of Elijah and show them this piece of bread I just got from a raven."

"Go for it, Bro!" John encouraged me.

We said goodbye to each other and hung up the phone. It was just getting dark when I longboarded out of the library parking lot with the piece of bread. There were a bunch of church buildings around. It didn't take long to find one with its front door wide open, looking welcoming and warm inside. I could tell that the service had already started, but I figured better late than never and walked into the tiny foyer. I placed my longboard against the wall, slipped in the quaint auditorium through the small double doors, and slid into a pew against the back wall of the church right next to the doors. Feeling like I was being inconspicuous enough, I set my backpack next to me on the pew and placed the bread from heaven beside it.

Now, from my point of view, I was simply enjoying a miraculous evening and looking forward to meeting some new people after the service and sharing my real-life Bible story with them. Glancing to my left across the middle aisle, I caught the eye of a little, old lady who gave me a warm smile. She seemed happy to see me. I looked back at the pastor and opened my Bible to the passage he was preaching from.

Maybe fifteen people scattered throughout the pews of the small auditorium; mostly everyone was older than me. Toward the front, a man and a few ladies occupied a couple pews on the left. He glanced at me a couple times, probably wondering who I was. Then he started whispering to the ladies next to him. I didn't pay much attention to them because I was focused on what the pastor was preaching, but one after the other, each lady stood up, walked down the aisle right past me, and exited the church. I didn't think anything of it at the time, assuming they were preparing something for after the service. It only dawned on me later that they were actually evacuating the building. I guess from their perspective, a strange, young man with a backpack was enough to cause alarm.

About five minutes later, I felt a tap on my shoulder. Turning around, I was more than surprised to see a police officer. In a hushed tone, he said, "May I have a word with you, sir?" Caught off guard, I slowly set my Bible next to me and got up. "Please bring your backpack with you," the officer said.

I grabbed my bag and Bible and followed him into the foyer. Then he said, "Can you step outside with me? I'm gonna need to see your ID." Stepping outside, I handed over my ID as he asked, "What are you doing at this church?"

"I was longboarding by and saw the front door opened with the lights on, so I went inside," I explained. "I thought everyone was welcome at church. Is everything OK?"

"Yes, everything is fine," he reassured me. "We got a call saying that a stranger had entered the church building with a backpack."

Another officer arrived and asked me to empty my backpack. I started laying my personal life out on the church's front lawn while they watched closely. First came my Bible, then two shirts, a pair of shorts, sandals, socks, and eventually even my underwear. They were thorough, so I kept going. Out came my charging cable, journal, pencil, safety vest, deodorant, toothbrush, and toothpaste. That was about it.

They then had me turn the backpack upside down and shake it. A few small items and some bits of trash fell onto the grass, but nothing dangerous. The first officer questioned why my ID said South Carolina when I was in Florida. I clarified that I was longboarding across America, having come from Miami. They didn't seem convinced.

A third police officer, much taller than the others, pulled up in his SUV. He was the sergeant, and the first officer quickly briefed him on the situation. When the sergeant heard that I was longboarding across America, he discouraged me from continuing the journey for some reason I can't remember. I paid little attention to his advice as he lacked full insight of my situation and didn't understand my deep determination to reach the Pacific Ocean.

As the police officers finished questioning me, the church service ended, and people started coming out of the building. The little, old lady remarked, "Oh, he wasn't hurtin' anyone. He was just followin' along with his Bible." As more people came out, they were looking at me and whispering to each other, curious to know what was going on. The pastor was the last to exit the building, and perhaps feeling compelled to address the situation, he stated, "Well, now that we know who you are, you're welcome here anytime." I didn't really know how to respond to that, so I simply replied, "Thanks."

I can understand why that church called the cops on me. Back in 2015, a man had walked into Bible study at a Methodist church in Charleston, South Carolina and tragically shot nine people, including the pastor. I guess I don't blame this little church in Live Oak for being suspicious of me. It must have seemed like a matter of life and death to them. In retrospect, I probably shouldn't have walked in late to a church I hadn't been to before. Then again, they left the church door wide open, as if to say, "Come on in!" It just never crossed my mind that a church would perceive me as a serious threat.

Since I had done nothing illegal, I was free to go. I grabbed my longboard and skated away in the dark, heading back to the house of a man who welcomed me without ever meeting me. I want to commend Bruce for this radical act of faith. He risked a lot by giving a complete stranger, who he had never even met, the keys to his house while being on the other side of the planet. This level of hospitality still blows my mind because I've never heard of anyone else doing something like that. To me, it feels like something Jesus would do.

As I longboarded closer to Bruce's house that night, I called Grandma Anna to update her on all the wild stories. She was amazed when I told her about the bird dropping me bread and shocked to hear that I had almost been arrested.

"Well, what did you do with the bread?" she asked.

"Oh no!" I exclaimed, suddenly realizing I'd left the bread on the pew in the church. The moment that officer tapped me on the shoulder, I completely forgot about it. Maybe whoever cleaned the church ate it and became a prophet. I guess I'll never know.

Central Florida brimmed with unexpected events and outcomes that taught me to live with courage and faith rather than worry and fear. Looking back, I can't help but see the hand of God in every moment from Victor's warmth and Turkish coffee to Kim picking me up on the side of the road to go to a concert. Time and again, when plans failed and the path ahead blurred, provision arrived. I used to think God's radical provision only happened in the Bible, but now I've seen it with my own eyes; He still provides in mysterious ways and uses anyone who is willing to be kind. Go ahead, put yourself out there! Perhaps you'll find that you're the next one to become someone's bread from heaven.

CHAPTER 5.

SOUTHERN HOSPITALITY AND NEW PERSPECTIVES

FEBRUARY 22 – MARCH 14, 2018

LIVE OAK, FLORIDA MOBILE, ALABAMA

I used to imagine that hospitality was just about kindness, but now I believe that it has the power to turn strangers into friends.

After staying at Bruce's house for three nights in Live Oak, I woke up early and set out for Tallahassee. The eighty-seven mile stretch ahead turned out to be one of the most enjoyable of my journey. The weather was perfect: clear skies, a light breeze, and just the right temperature. The roads were freshly paved with little traffic, making the ride smooth and effortless. But what made the day truly special was the landscape. Towering live oak trees lined Highway 90, their sprawling branches draped in Spanish moss, creating a scene that felt unmistakably like the Deep South.

Along the way, I passed a few horse ranches, their elegant white fences enclosing vast fields where graceful horses galloped freely. As I neared Lake Miccosukee, I slowed to take in the sight of bald cypress trees rising from the swampy waters, their intricate root systems weaving in and out above the surface of the water. The beauty of it all made the miles pass quickly. By the time I reached Tallahassee, the sun was setting behind me, casting a golden glow across the city, while the moon rose over the eastern horizon. I pushed toward the west side of town, where I had reserved a night at the Sun and Moon Hostel on Day Street.

The ride was the farthest I had traveled in a single day. Along the way, I had met a homeless traveler named Kalico and his girlfriend, Brook. They stood on a median at a stoplight, holding a cardboard sign and hoping for spare change. Instead of skating past, I stopped to sit with Kalico for a while. We talked about life on the road, and, at some point, I asked if he had ever heard of Jesus. He nodded, and we spoke about Jesus for a bit before I eventually said goodbye and continued on toward the hostel.

When I arrived at the hostel, a woman named Lauren greeted me at the door. There was something special about the place. It had warmth to it, the kind of energy that made it feel like home. Everyone there had a story, a unique journey that had somehow led them all to this shared space on the same night.

Antone was one of the first people I met. He had a way of making people feel seen, asking thoughtful questions and laughing easily. I admired that about him and hoped to be more like that myself. Then there was Freddie, a girl from Germany who spent a lot of time journaling, much like I did. Joe, a web designer, had just been let go from NASA in Boston. When they fired him, he said he smoked a joint and hit the road. Edmond, originally from the Philippines, had studied at Northwestern Illinois and had just arrived in Tallahassee to begin a doctoral program.

It was crazy how all our lives had intersected at this little hostel. That night, we made tacos together and sat around the table sharing stories. It wasn't just the meal that filled the room: it was the sense of community, of travelers from different walks of life coming together, if only for a night. When it was time to sleep, I found a bunk in a room with three other travelers. It wasn't going to be the most comfortable night, but it was better than sleeping outside on cardboard. Staying in a place like this, connecting with strangers, hearing their stories, and breaking bread together, felt so much richer than the solitude of a hotel room. After finishing my journal entry for the night, I put my pencil away, lay down on my bunk bed, and fell asleep.

The next day, a Couchsurfing host in Chattahoochee, Florida, accepted my couch request. The small town sat just south of the Florida-Georgia line, and by noon, I was back on the road.

When I arrived, my host, Gene, greeted me with a warm smile, eager to show me the pot of shrimp gumbo he had been slow-cooking all day. The moment I walked through the front door, the smell of simmering spices and seafood filled the air. If I hadn't already known I was in the South, that first bite of gumbo sealed the deal. Gene was the definition of southern hospitality: welcoming, kind, and a great cook. After a long day of travel, that meal was one of the best things I had ever tasted.

While I was eating, Gene told me, "I just want to let you know that I am polyamorous. Do you know what that means?"

"Uhh, no. Sorry, I'm not exactly sure," I responded.

He explained, "It means that I have a romantic relationship with multiple women. Right now, I have two. They are both fully aware, and they also have other boyfriends, so it's all good. By the way, one is coming over right now, and then we're going out, so I'll be back later tonight. Feel free to relax, watch TV, and use the shower. You can sleep on the couch in the living room, and if the dog is lying there, just push him off. I've put a pillow and blanket there for you to use."

"Wow, Gene, thanks. I really appreciate you letting me spend a couple nights here," I said.

I was continually amazed by the hospitality, generosity, and trusting spirit of Gene. He was so nice and friendly to everyone, no matter who they were. It's probably part of the reason that so many girls loved him. I had heard of open relationships like this before, but I had never personally met someone who was involved in them. So, I was introduced to one of his girlfriends the first night, and the second one the next day. I had quality conversations with them, and they were both very friendly and kind; I didn't look down on them or treat them any differently. During my trip, I actually enjoyed staying with all kinds of hosts, even if they were dissimilar to me. If they had good hosting reviews on the app, then I would stay with them.

I was only planning to be in Chattahoochee for two nights, but because there were thunderstorms, the day I was supposed to leave, I ended up staying one more day. While it rained outside, I was inside trying to find my next host. After a good deal of messaging back and forth, Martin from Panama City confirmed that he could host me for two nights. I had no idea at the time that he was a satanist, but it always felt good when a host accepted my request. The next day, I longboarded to Martin's apartment, but I won't retell the story (as you already read earlier).

After I left Martin's place, I had a handful of Couchsurfing experiences across the Panhandle of Florida. The first guy was a simple dude who had traveled a big circle around the US after losing his family long before most do. His name was Clinton, and he just started walking and never looked back. By the time I met him, he had already yoyoed the Appalachian Trail and walked across America multiple times. When he wasn't traveling, he resided in Panama City Beach, which is where he hosted me in his simple single-level flat right on the Gulf Coast, overlooking the water. It was probably the most peaceful place I've stayed in my life.

Tony, my next host, had come to Florida for a girl and started a business; he ended up losing the girl but kept his business. He made food adhering to the Paleo diet. Tony had lots of bone broth in his house and tons of meat in the freezer. I jokingly called him a paleontologist and went to the farmers' market with him to help him sell his almond butter. He was a funny guy, and when it came time for me to leave, Tony grabbed his skateboard and cruised down the road with me to send me off.

My next host was a single mom from Australia. When I received her confirmation, she gave me the address to her house and told me that she and her son wouldn't be home for a couple hours, but I was welcome to let myself in, watch TV, and take a shower if I wanted. It was a strange feeling to be relaxing in the home of someone I had never met, but it wasn't the first time, and I was kind of getting used to it. When she and her son finally arrived home, I stood up and greeted them in the kitchen.

"Hey, I'm Daniel. You must be Sacha and Boaz."

"It's great to meet you, Daniel," Sacha said with a beautiful Australian accent. Her son Boaz was a bit shy at first but that wore off in about five minutes, especially after he said, "Hey, do you wanna see the fort we built in the backyard?"

I wasn't gonna say no to that, so I followed Boaz and Sacha out to the backyard where the edge of the woods started. A set of planks had been secured on top of wooded pilings, making a boardwalk that went straight through the woods and over the brush conveniently avoiding the swampy ground. Boaz was running ahead of me on the skinny boards with no fear of falling, as if he had done this hundreds of times. After walking several yards on the boardwalk, the woods opened up to a really cool fort that had a roof, a mosquito net, and a hammock for relaxing. I had great fun with Sacha and Boaz and stayed with them a few nights.

One thing that surprised me about Sacha was how many Couchsurfing reviews she had as a single mother. It was over a hundred, which meant that she had more than that number of guests come through her house. I asked if she had ever had any bad experiences, and she said that she hadn't had one. It was her way of showing Boaz the cultures of the world, as she had hosted people from all over the globe.

After leaving Sacha and Boaz's house in Northwest Florida, I began longboarding to the next host's house in Mobile, Alabama. I remember the day that I crossed the state line. It was a beautiful sunny day and a bit chilly, perfect for longboarding. It was an eventful moment for me because the Florida-Alabama state line was the first border I crossed out of seven while on my longboard trip. It gave me so much confidence and courage to continue onward. I started a new tradition at each border by taking a picture of myself standing next to the "Welcome" sign of each new state.

Alabama's coast was attractive, and the weather was the perfect temperature, but there was a head wind blowing toward me that made it harder to move forward. Sometimes it would blow so hard that if I didn't keep pushing forward, it would take me backward. I was wondering why it couldn't be blowing in the direction I was moving. I was getting a little tired of the wind as I longboarded down the highway when a man on a recumbent bike began to ride next to me.

"Hey there! Where ya headed?" he called out to me.

I told him that I was going to California, and he was really impressed. His name was Al, like the first two letters of Alabama. He rode next to me for a while as we both continued down Highway 180 paralleling the Gulf Shores coast. I found out that he had accomplished many cross-country journeys in his life with his bicycle, and he was intrigued by my journey as well. We talked about the weather, our travels, and Dauphin Island, which was the place we both were heading for. Because Al was so fond of me, he offered to pull me with his bike as I held onto the back of his seat. We cruised down the road as I held on with a big smile on my face. I thought it was so funny that he would let me skitch on the back of his bike. Eventually, we came to the end of the road where there was a ferry that would take us across the water to Dauphin Island. As I stood on the deck of the ferry, the water around me glistened from the light beams of the sun. I took a deep breath of the cool ocean breeze and felt at peace when I released it.

After the ferry dropped us off, I said goodbye to Al, and we wished each other a safe journey. Then I continued longboarding down the road and followed it to a bridge that brought me to the mainland of Alabama; I was now in Mobile County. Al had informed me that many cross-country cyclists used this route to move east and west across America. I had never done much research on how to travel across America on a bike or skateboard, so I was happy to find out that I was on the same route that others have been using for years.

I learned that many cyclists take this route to avoid going through the busy city of Mobile because some drivers are not always friendly to bicyclists, and it can make for a dangerous situation. Mobile is the fourth most populated city in the state, and for a while, I pronounced it, "mobile" like a mobile phone, but the locals pronounce it, "MOH-beel," which rhymes with Tar Heel.

My next host lived in the suburbs of the city, which was about twenty-six miles north of my current location. He was so thoughtful that he asked me if I would like him to pick me up with his car. I responded that it would be much appreciated, but I would need to be dropped back off in this exact spot so that I wouldn't skip a single mile of the journey. He agreed and told me that he was on his way. Soon enough, a vehicle pulled off to the side of the road; I knew it was him. He rolled down the window and said, "Hey, are you Daniel?"

"Yeah!" I responded.

"Jump on in! It's really nice to meet you. I'm Matt," he said as I opened the car door. His daughter, Phoebe, was in the vehicle too. She was young and calm with thin hair and would often ask her dad questions. As we drove down the road, I noticed Matt was playing Christian music on the radio. I found out that he followed Jesus and had studied at a college of theology in Wales; this brought up some good discussion about theology as I had graduated from a Bible college. We enjoyed our conversation with an occasional question from Phoebe, as we traveled back to his house.

When we arrived, I was welcomed by Matt's wife, Rachel, and their younger son, Reuben. They were a family of four from the United Kingdom living in Southern Alabama. Reuben had the cutest British accent, which was very different from the accent of most Alabamians. I was given a comfortable couch to sleep on and after taking a hot shower, I fell right asleep.

The next morning, Rachel told me that Matt had left for work, and she was about to leave with the kids. "We'll be back later this afternoon," she added. "Make yourself at home, and feel free to help yourself to the breakfast items in the kitchen."

After they left, I made myself a delicious breakfast sandwich with a fried egg between a toasted bagel. Again I was impressed that they would leave me alone in their house and trust me enough to be there. I think they could tell that I was a good person, and I was sure that they had read most, if not all, of my reviews on the Couchsurfing app. Then I relaxed around the house and did some reading.

When they all returned home, Matt was excited to tell me that they would be having a BBQ and bonfire that evening with some friends from their church and neighbors who were immigrants from Iraq. That night, Matt made a mouth-watering BBQ, and I helped build the bonfire. It was fun to meet and interact with people from different cultures and countries. We all enjoyed a great night full of good fun, great food, roasted marshmallows, and lots of laughter.

The following day was Saturday and also Matt's twin nieces' birthday. Matt and Rachel had planned to travel to their relatives' house who lived in Pensacola to attend the party and said I was welcome to join them. It was about a one-hour drive back to the city that I had recently longboarded from. While we were in the car, I remember thinking to myself, *What took me all day to travel by longboard just took us one hour by car.* So, to me, it felt like we got there in no time at all. We pulled up to a nice one-story house, and as we all got out of the car, their family came out to greet us. Everyone was giving hugs and kisses. The whole family felt warm, friendly, and welcoming, especially to me.

After helping to unload the car, I began getting to know some of the relatives. They offered me a drink, gave me a chair to relax in, and started asking me questions to get to know me better. The vibe of the house was in full celebration mode, but, within a matter of minutes, everything shifted.

Phoebe started having a seizure. Because it was minor, it wasn't as obvious to everyone at first, but Rachel and Matt immediately knew what was happening to her. Some people started acting anxiously when they realized what was taking place. We could all tell that this was painful for the sweet girl and her parents, but there wasn't much that any of us could do. I watched Matt and Rachel handle the unfortunate situation systematically.

It was clear that they were concerned for their daughter's health, but they remained calm the whole time as if they weren't surprised by the situation. I soon discovered that this was a common occurrence for their daughter because she had a rare condition called SMART (stroke migraines after radiotherapy) which developed after the radiotherapy she received for her cancerous brain tumor. An extremely rare condition, even amongst those who've had cranial radiation.

I felt so bad and was heartbroken for them as I began to watch their day of celebration turn into disaster. Their plan was to quickly take her to the hospital to get checked out, so we all got back into the car, except Reuben, who stayed at their relative's house. I sat in the front passenger seat as Rachel held her daughter in the back. Matt began to rush us to the hospital, and when we got to the highway, he turned on his hazard lights and cautiously cruised well over the speed limit because time was of the essence. If we got stuck behind a vehicle in front of us, he would continue honking until they moved over because this was an emergency. I could see the love these two parents had for their precious daughter.

As we sped down I-10, I realized that we were headed back toward Mobile. I thought that we would go to the Pensacola hospital, but Matt informed me, "There's no doctors that know our daughter better than the ones in Mobile, so that's why we are going back there."

"Are you worried that you may get pulled over by the police for speeding?" I asked. Matt responded, "It would be better if they did, so that we could get a police escort the rest of the way."

They knew they would be spending the night at the hospital and wouldn't be able to host me like they were planning, so they ended up calling one of their friends who also hosted through the Couchsurfing app. He lived in Mobile too, and after being informed of the situation, he was happy to host me at his place.

His name was Mike, and we had an incredible time together and great conversations. He showed me some really nice spots within the city, including the Battle House Renaissance Hotel. The architecture of this hotel was immaculate; the building was full of history. When we got back to his house, I was fully impressed. The whole house was finely decorated, and I got my own private bedroom with a queen-sized bed, clean bed sheets, and a big fluffy comforter. I was feeling tired, and the bed was looking so comfortable, so I went straight to sleep.

The next morning, Mike asked me, "Do you want to go to Starbucks?"

"I would love to," I responded. So, he brought me to Starbucks and graciously paid for my drink. I was beyond grateful for his kind-hearted southern hospitality, but he could only host me for one night, so Mike made a phone call to another Couchsurfing host named David who also lived in Mobile. It was Sunday morning, so David picked me up on the way to his local church. We immediately made a strong connection, and I knew that David was a great person. His church was also welcoming and friendly. I met his wife, Jillian, and their daughters after the service, and then he offered to lend me his car so that I could drive to a café and explore Mobile a little bit more. I hadn't even known David for more than four hours, but our connection was so strong that he trusted me and my driving skills enough to give me the keys to his car.

I drove to a coffee shop to spend some time reading and journaling. Driving felt a bit strange after having traveled exclusively by longboard since Miami, but I was fine. Later that evening, I returned to meet David and Jillian's family for tacos. After dinner, we headed over to an apartment complex where refugees from various countries were living. David and Jillian often visited to provide food, supplies, and friendship. As soon as we arrived, a group of kids surrounded us, laughing and running around. I jumped in to play with them, and before long, we were all dancing together, caught up in the simple joy of the moment.

On Monday night, they were having a small group meeting at their friend's house with some people from their local church, and I joined them. We all had a blast that night playing horseshoe, conversing around a firepit, and eating delicious food. When we got back to the house, everyone said good night and went off to bed, but David stayed up with me to finish a conversation we had started. I don't remember all the words that were spoken, but I do remember David explaining why he was so kind and generous to others and hospitable to all the travelers that stayed in his home. He said something like, "It's because I have experienced the love of Jesus in my life. His love for me helps me to love my wife, daughters, neighbors, church family, and any strangers I meet along the way. My life before wasn't as sweet as it is now since encountering the love of Jesus."

One way that both David and Jillian showed their love for others was with their encouraging words. After I left, they gave me one of the nicest Couchsurfing reviews that still encourages me to this day. Their words spoke life to me and motivated me to keep going. This is what they said:

> *Daniel is as genuine and admirable as any surfer we have ever hosted. He has a very real faith which produces an authenticity and meekness not readily found in everyday life. I have watched as Daniel has very naturally fit into about any environment and people group he is connected with (adults, children, strangers, people of different faith, refugees, etc.). He is on an incredible journey longboarding across the US and has some of the most hilarious and inspiring stories that you just have to hear to believe. In the few short days that our family has gotten to know Daniel, there is a very easy and natural trust with him. Daniel is very quick to help out with anything that is needed. He is very polite and respectful in all circumstances. Our family is blessed to have had these last few days with Daniel and believe no doubt that if you open your home to Daniel, you'll encounter the same (if not greater) blessing along the way. Peace, brother! You're welcome back anytime!*

Couchsurfing reviews can be read by anyone, and it is how other hosts decide if they will let you stay at their house. If you receive a review like this, it will greatly increase your chances of being hosted by others, which is why I was beyond grateful for this review and the two other great reviews I received from Matt and Mike. Mobile, Alabama seriously impressed me by the hospitality, friendliness, and generosity of this incredible community and the three sweet homes and families who welcomed me.

I wondered when this hospitality would end, and then I received another notification on my phone from the Couchsurfing app saying that Will from Biloxi, Mississippi "Accepted your request" on March 13, 2018. My plan was to leave early the next morning; David was headed to work in the morning, so they decided that Jillian would drive me back to the same spot where Matt and Phoebe had originally picked me up. I said goodbye to David before I left and got in the car with Jillian and her daughters, who piled in the backseat.

As we drove, I began to think about all the new friends I had made through Northern Florida and Alabama from Gene and Tony to Mike and Matt. I thought about the countless meals, stories, and rides that had all come my way. Deep gratefulness flooded over me for the southern hospitality that had welcomed me in. By the time Jillian had pulled over, I felt the Spirit reveal a truth to me about hospitality: *It really has the power to turn strangers into friends.* With that realization, I hopped out of the car and said farewell to the family. I put my board down and started pushing west toward Mississippi on Alabama's Costal Connection—Highway 188.

CHAPTER 6.

COASTAL ADVENTURES WITH CAPTAIN WILL

MARCH 14 – MAY 1, 2018

MOBILE, ALABAMA TO BILOXI, MISSISSIPPI

I used to imagine that some places weren't worth exploring, but now I believe that every place holds hidden adventures if you'll just learn to look.

"Whad'ya think, Daniel?"

"This is incredible! I've never experienced anything like this before," I exclaimed.

"Good, I'm glad you're enjoy it out here," Will responded. "Now, we have to follow this river for a few miles before we reach the Gulf Coast. There's a drawbridge coming up, and I need to radio the operator."

I was on a ship in Mississippi with my new friend, Will. We were headed out to the Gulf Coast for the day to pick up some bulldozers stranded on an offshore island. Just then, Captain Will picked up his radio and switched to Channel 13. "CSX Biloxi, this is the Longbay," he called. No response. He repeated the call once more before a voice finally crackled through.

"This is CSX Biloxi. Go ahead."

"We are an outbound vessel requesting an opening."

"Yes, sir, Captain. We'll get 'er open for you right now."

"Thank you very much. Longbay standing by on one-three."

This meant that Will would keep his radio on Channel 13, maintaining communication as we approached the bridge. Once we passed through, he switched back to Channel 16, the universal hailing and distress channel monitored by all vessels.

I listened, catching bits of sea captain jargon as Captain Will steered us forward. I had seen drawbridges open from land before but experiencing it from the water was something else entirely. The massive steel arms slowly lifted on either side, clearing a path for our ship as we cruised beneath. For the first time, I saw the waterways through the eyes of those who relied on them.

As we approached the open sea, we glided past the towering casinos lining the Biloxi shore. Will shared tales of his experiences over the years working on these waters. As I looked out the windows of the pilot house, I could see the deck of the ship two stories below me. This particular ship was a landing craft; it looked similar to the famous amphibious seacrafts used in World War II to transport infantry from the big battleships to the beaches of Normandy, but this one that Will owned was much bigger. It was designed to carry large equipment like military tanks, vehicles, and bulldozers across the sea and drop them off on almost any beach. It could tread in shallow waters and lower its front gate, which would turn into a ramp to pick up and drop off almost any vehicle.

"Are you getting hungry yet?" Will asked me. It was about 7 a.m. by this time.

"Yeah, I would love to eat something."

"Well, why don't you go down to the galley and cook us up some pancakes? There should be some pancake mix in one of the cabinets and all the other ingredients there too."

I quickly responded, "That sounds great!" and made my way back down the stairs to whip up some pancakes. I descended a couple of flights before finding a hallway with a few doors. One was labeled Galley, and when I stepped inside, I found a small kitchen with aluminum pots and pans hanging from hooks on the walls and ceiling. The roar of the ship's engines filled the space, making everything vibrate slightly.

Making pancakes on a moving ship was an entirely new challenge. Nothing stayed still. I figured that if I just got all the ingredients into one big bowl, the ship would mix it for me. The griddle, the cooking utensils, even the batter swayed with the rhythm of the sea, forcing me to adjust my balance with every movement. But before long, I had a towering stack of pancakes ready, along with paper plates, plastic utensils, maple syrup, and a good-sized jar of peanut butter.

I carried it all back up to the pilot house, where Will and I dug in. Compared to the noisy, vibrating galley, the pilot house felt calm and quiet, with the steady hum of the ship blending into the open ocean around us. The only other deckhand on board mostly kept to himself and had no interest in breakfast. As we ate, I looked out the windows. Water stretched endlessly in every direction, the horizon blurring into the sky. I had never been this far out on the ocean before, and the vastness of it all was both humbling and exhilarating.

"Hey Daniel," Will said. "If you look up ahead, you might be able to spot the island we're looking for. Do you see it?"

"Yeah, I think so!"

"Can you see the two small objects moving across the island?" Will was pointing out the bulldozers, which we were going to pick up. It was his job to bring them back to the mainland because they were due for some maintenance. He began giving commands to his deckhand to drop the front gate. We pulled right up to the edge of the island and dropped the gate directly on the beach, then used it as a bridge for the two huge bulldozers.

For Will, this was just another ordinary day, but to me, this was an extraordinary opportunity. *How in the world did I get here?* I thought. *I left Florida on a longboard a few months ago, and now I'm on a ship in the Gulf Coast picking up bulldozers with someone who is basically a stranger to me.* By this time, I had gotten used to being with strangers. I had stayed with roughly eighteen hosts as I made my way through Florida and Alabama. Sometimes we can be scared or intimidated by strangers, but the truth is that everyone who has a friend used to know them as a stranger. Now, I'm not saying to trust every stranger, but I've learned that sometimes a stranger can be the one to open up a world of new adventures for you. And in this moment, I was on a phenomenal adventure with a stranger who was becoming my friend.

Mississippi held an air of mystery for me. I had never set foot in this state, and perhaps, subconsciously, I harbored stereotypes about the people who lived there—imagining thick Southern drawls and guys who chewed on straw and tobacco. I was eager to uncover its secrets, but I didn't expect to stay in Mississippi for more than a few days.

Longboarding in the southern heat was even less comfortable than waking up before sunrise. Although I loved sleeping in, I learned to start my days early, determined not to miss out on the cool morning air that made traveling so much easier. I settled into a routine, hitting the road around 4:30 a.m. and riding until about 10:30 or 11 a.m. After a short lunch break, I'd push through the afternoon, gritting my teeth through the heat to cover a few more miles.

On Wednesday, March 14, 2018, after Jillian and her daughters dropped me off, I followed Highway 188 until I reached Highway 90, which led me to the next state. I reached the Alabama–Mississippi border and snapped a picture in front of the "Welcome to Mississippi" sign at 12:08 p.m. The sky was a perfect, cloudless blue, and the sun lit up everything around me. Cruising along the busy stretch of Highway 90, the pavement curved gently through the pine trees that lined both sides of the road. Their tall, slender trunks reached high above me, swaying just slightly in the breeze. It wasn't too hot yet, just warm enough to keep me comfortable in a hoodie and my safety vest. When I saw the big red, white, and blue welcome sign with "Birthplace of America's Music" written underneath, I couldn't help but smile. I was officially in my third state and thrilled that I had made it this far.

I had been messaging back and forth with Will, who I would soon meet. I told him that I expected to arrive in the late afternoon. That day, I longboarded around 55 miles (88 kilometers) and came into Ocean Springs on Highway 90, also known as Bienville Boulevard. Will was on his way back from picking up his youngest daughter from a school event, so he offered to pick me up on his way home. I explained that I would accept only if he would be willing to drop me off in the same spot when it was time for me to depart. He messaged me back and let me know that he would be more than happy to do that for me. Then Will told me he could pick me up off Bienville Boulevard and gave me the description of his truck. It wasn't long before I spotted his vehicle, and Will spotted me.

"Hey there! You must be Daniel," Will said with a big smile as he was getting out of his truck to shake my hand.

I extended my hand and responded, "That's right, and you must be Will. It's nice to meet you."

Will greeted me with a firm, welcoming handshake and a bright, easygoing smile. He stood about my height, 5"10', with a slender build, short brown hair neatly combed, and a clean-shaven face that made him look both sharp and approachable. He dressed in a tucked-in button-down and slacks, a look that fit his polished but relaxed personality. From the start, I could tell he was observant and inquisitive without being pushy, and his confident voice carried a friendly, upbeat tone that immediately put me at ease. As I climbed into the passenger seat of his truck, he introduced me to his daughter, Aubrey. She was nine years old with long blonde hair and a playful spark in her eyes. Sitting in the middle of the back seat, she peppered me with questions about my trip. Clearly, she wasn't shy, and the genuine curiosity she shared with her dad made our ride feel warm and familiar, like I was already part of the family.

After a fifteen-minute drive, we arrived at their white-and-yellow house that rested on wooden pilings to prevent it from flooding during the rainy season. The house sat a full story above the ground so that the truck could easily park underneath the house. It was located right next to the Tchoutacabouffa River (sorry, I don't know how to pronounce it either) with a large green lawn in the backyard sitting between the house and the edge of the water. We unloaded from the truck and walked up a set of twelve stairs to get inside their home.

"I've never been in a house on stilts before," I told Will.

"Well, it definitely helps keep the water out during the rainy season and the stairs keep me young," Will responded. "I had to renovate this house after Hurricane Katrina came through several years ago. The water was so high that it covered the kitchen counter. You could float a kayak through the living room!" That was hard for me to believe, since we were already so far off the ground, but Will had done a good job of restoring the place. The house was nice and homey with wood flooring and lots of windows to let the natural light come through. The kitchen window faced the backyard, where I could see the river and a decent-sized boat docked on the edge of the water. While I was looking at the boat, his oldest daughter, Juliana, who was twelve, walked in. She had long dark hair and was more reserved than Aubrey.

Will introduced me to Juliana and then said, "Hey girls, why don't we show Daniel where he will be staying while he's here?" The girls hurried to put their shoes on and then walked with me through the back door of the house. They led me down the stairs of the porch and across the grass to the vintage-looking yacht that was roughly thirty-five feet long. Painted on the stern of the boat were the words *The Interlude*. Will explained all the details and rules of the boat and let me know that I was welcome to stay here. I was thrilled because I had never spent the night on a boat, and I had no idea that this was where I would be sleeping.

That evening, Will invited me into their home to have dinner with them, and we had a great night of conversation. I learned that Juliana liked reading books, being on the water, and hanging out with her dad. Aubrey loved to sing, dance, jump on their trampoline, and eat chocolate chip cookies. I learned that Will had gone through a divorce a few years earlier but had been granted custody of his daughters. It's uncommon for most fathers in similar cases, yet his good character and integrity had made the difference. He loved spending as much time with his daughters as possible, and he also loved being on the water.

When we finished eating dinner, Will had the girls serve dessert, and we all had a sweet time getting to know each other. I learned that Will had served as a civilian captain on an active-duty oceanographic ship. It wasn't a combat vessel, but it was serious work out at sea. He had spent years on the water and had plenty of stories to share. Farther down the river, he owned another property with a dock where he kept a couple of boats, a ship, and a variety of equipment. The ocean wasn't just part of his past; it was a central part of his life.

Before I turned in for the night, Will told me I could stay as long as I needed. I usually kept moving after a few days or a week, but something about this stop felt different. Will was always working on a project or heading into something interesting, and he never hesitated to include me. There was always another adventure around the corner. The next one was the trip out to sea to pick up a pair of bulldozers. When he invited me to join, I didn't think twice.

Every day brought something new, and before I knew it, I kept extending my stay. Whether it was a small project or an unexpected adventure, I was always up for it, and Will noticed. At one point, he half-joked that I should just move to Biloxi, saying we made a great team and that it was rare to find someone willing to jump in and help with anything. We hadn't even scratched the surface of everything we'd end up doing together, but it was already clear we clicked. He was always fixing, building, planning, or hauling something. Every day felt like I was stepping into a new episode of "Coastal Adventures with Captain Will."

One day after picking up Aubrey and Juliana from school, Will took us to a spot that was overgrown with blackberry bushes. Armed with clear plastic bags, we began a friendly race to see who could harvest the most. By the end, our bags were overflowing, and our tongues were stained purple from gulping down the delicious berries. After the harvest, we capped off the day by baking a mouth-watering blackberry pie for dessert, and we served the warm pie with a cold scoop of vanilla ice cream.

Will was also very involved in his community, and whatever the event, Will would always ask if I wanted to join them. One time, Will was asked to be the announcer for the basketball game at his daughters' school, and I got to help run the clock and scoreboard. Will introduced me to so many people from their local community; it seemed like he knew everyone. Even when we drove around town, he would tell me the name of the person walking on the sidewalk or driving by. Will even knew the former mayor of Ocean Springs and was invited to her mother's birthday party one Sunday afternoon. They said I was welcome to come too, so I tagged along with Will and had a great time.

Another day it was raining so hard outside that a large puddle began forming in the backyard, but rainy days didn't discourage Will. "Hey girls!" he exclaimed. "Let's see if Daniel's balance is as good as mine! Come on!" We all followed Will down the stairs as the rain poured off the roof. We watched him look for something in the utility room underneath the house. The room was pretty disorganized, so it took him a few minutes, but eventually he exclaimed, "Here it is!" Will held up a skimboard in his hands, which was something like a small surfboard.

"You see that big puddle?" Will said with a grin. "We're gonna see who can skim the farthest across it."

The rules were simple and ridiculous, just how Will liked them. You had to sprint full speed, drop the skimboard at the edge of the puddle, jump on, and ride it across without wiping out. Will went first, eager to show off his technique. To my surprise, he actually pulled it off—at first. He glided across the water with impressive balance, like a man born for puddle sports … until he fell.

Halfway through, he leaned too far back, lost his footing, and landed flat on his back right in the middle of the puddle. Water flew everywhere. He stood up dripping and laughing, soaked from head to toe. But if you ask Will, he'll swear it was me who took the fall. According to him, he skimmed across the water perfectly, and I was the one who got soaked. But you can believe who you want.

Will really loved Aubrey and Juliana. He was always looking out for them and finding ways to make good memories and have fun. Will was young at heart and had no problem keeping up with his daughters. I was impressed by his parenting and also his positivity; he could pick out the good in every situation. Even though he had had his fair share of difficulties, there was no trace of bitterness or disappointment that I could see. He just loved being alive and spending quality time with his girls and making the most of every situation. His positive attitude made me enjoy being around him.

Days went by so quickly at Will's house because they were always full of fun things to do. Every Thursday morning, we would all wake up a little earlier so we could go to the local donut shop, TatoNut, before dropping Aubrey and Juliana off at school. This donut shop was our favorite. Their donuts are delicious because they are made with potato flour which makes them moist and chewy. I started looking forward to Thursday mornings while I stayed at Will's place.

With Couchsurfing, I never wanted to overstay my welcome, plus I was trying to make it across America. But Will and I got along so well, and Aubrey and Juliana made it clear that they didn't want me to go. They started saying stuff like, "Why don't you just build a tiny house in the backyard and live here?" We were having so much fun together, plus I was learning so much from being with them.

Will always had things that needed to get done, and I didn't mind helping him because he was providing three meals a day and a place to sleep; for me, this was a good enough trade. I always wanted to do my best to be a person who contributed, not just consumed. If I saw something that needed to be cleaned, I would just clean it. After meals, I would take the initiative to do the dishes and bring out the trash. If I noticed something was unorganized in the house, I'd ask them where it was supposed to go and then put it away.

Will would tell me how helpful it was to have me around because in just a few weeks, he would be hosting his big, annual Easter BBQ party at the house with around sixty guests. There was a lot to do to get ready for the big day. So, I pitched in by power-washing the porch, cutting the grass, fixing the toilet, and organizing cabinets, the laundry room, and that utility room under the house. Then I power-washed the garage floor and driveway, fixed a part of the roof, did some work on the boat, and even painted all the walls below the house. All that work paid off, and the Easter BBQ party was a big success.

Before the party, Will had connected with some businessmen in the Bahamas who were interested in purchasing one of his ships. After the party, he decided to plan a short two-day business trip to meet with them and, as a thank-you for all my help, paid for my flight to come along. I was thrilled. Thankfully, I had my passport, and everything seemed set for an unforgettable adventure. But the night before our flight, while checking in online, Will realized his passport had expired. He stared at the screen in disbelief. The tickets were non-refundable, and it was too late to fix the issue. He told me I should go without him, but I didn't feel right about that. I asked Will if I could pray with him that night, and we did. "There's probably a better reason why things turned out this way," I said. Will appreciated the perspective, and we both went to bed with a little more peace than we expected.

Now that Easter had come, spring break was in full swing. The girls were on a break from school, which meant another adventure. "Each year," Will began to explain, "one of the girls joins me on a fun trip while the other stays with her mom. This time, it's Juliana's turn, and I've got an idea that involves you, Daniel."

Curious, I asked, "What's your plan?"

"Well, Juliana and I dreamt of riding a jet ski from the start of the Mississippi River to the Gulf of Mexico, but it's too long for Easter break. Instead, we'll explore the Suwannee River in Florida. It starts in the Okefenokee National Wildlife Refuge in Georgia and ends at the Gulf Coast, with amazing freshwater springs along the way. We'll be doing a stretch in Florida, and we want you to come. We have an extra tent. The Suwannee is fed by many freshwater springs in North Florida, so while we'll take the jet ski down the river each day, you can explore all the springs. Each night, we will reconvene and set up our campsite."

The plan was for me to drive the truck during the day and explore the springs while they jetted down the river. Will would send me a location pin of a boat launch where I would pick them up, and then we would find a camp spot for the night.

Will pulled out his phone and started showing me pictures of the springs; they were truly stunning. How could I pass up that opportunity? Just a few days after Easter, excitement filled the air as we prepared for the trip. We had the truck packed in no time flat. I helped load the kayak and camping gear in the bed of the truck while Will hooked up the trailer with the jet ski loaded on top. On April 4, we set off for another adventure, bound for the Suwannee River in Northern Florida.

During the drive, I reflected on the unexpected turns since arriving in Mississippi. Originally, I never expected to stay more than a few days in Biloxi, nor could I have imagined I'd be driving back to Florida on a family vacation. The five-and-a-half-hour road trip was filled with conversation, car games, and scenic views. Before we knew it, we reached the Dowling Park Boat Ramp near the familiar town of Live Oak where I had that police encounter. It was just before sunset, and we set up our tents right next to the river and enjoyed a delicious dinner of leftover Easter BBQ brisket and Hawaiian rolls. Then we turned into our tents for the night and slept beneath the stars.

The next morning, we rose early, packed up our tents, backed up the trailer down the boat ramp, and pushed the jet ski into the river. Will strapped down a couple gas tanks, packed food and water, and loaded extra supplies for their day trip. He handed me the keys to his truck and said, "Have fun! We'll see you later tonight." This was the second time someone had given me the keys to their vehicle while I was on this trip, and it wouldn't be the last. I was always surprised by the amount of trust that people had with me driving their vehicles, especially with a trailer, but it was nice to have some freedom to do as I pleased.

After Will secured everything on the jet ski, Juliana joined him. They departed down the Suwannee River while I waved goodbye, looking forward to the adventures the day would hold. I ended up driving south to Branford, parked the truck, and paddled up the Suwannee River to the Little River Spring. I texted Will my location, and they met me there on the jet ski. We swam in the clear blue cove of the spring and had a wonderful time. Then Will told me to hook the kayak up to the back of the jet ski, and they jetted me back down river, where we explored the spring at Ivey Memorial Park. Finally, Will and Juliana continued on down the river. That evening, I picked them up from a boat launch Will had sent me the coordinates of—they had covered around 25 miles (40 kilometers). Then we went to the Suwannee Cove campground just south of Branford, where Will had reserved a camp spot for us earlier that day.

Because we were so close to Live Oak, Florida, I reached out to that Couchsurfing host, Bruce, who graciously let me stay at his house while he was in Australia. It had been roughly two months since I had last messaged him. Now that he was back from his trip Down Under, I asked if he would want to meet Will, Juliana, and me at a restaurant in Branford. Excited by the idea, Bruce eagerly agreed, so we found a little restaurant that was central for all of us. As we pulled into the parking lot, I spotted Bruce; it was like his profile pictures had come to life. Walking over, I extended my hand, feeling as if things were coming full circle.

"Nice to finally meet you, Daniel," Bruce said with a smile on his face as we shook hands.

"It's great meeting you too, Bruce. It's nice to be able to greet you in person and thank you for letting me stay at your house," I said.

"It wasn't a problem for me, and I'm glad you were able to stay."

I introduced Bruce to Will and Juliana, who were just as happy to meet him. Dinner was filled with good stories from Bruce's travels to Australia. Then Will shared stories about when he took both his daughters to Australia. He continued to surprise me with stories of all his travels with his daughters, including France and Israel. We had such a nice visit; it was like hanging out with old friends.

The morning of April 7 was especially exciting. Will and Juliana were planning to make it all the way to Suwannee, Florida, where the river meets the Gulf of Mexico. They had been averaging about 27 miles (43 kilometers) a day, and this was the final stretch. As we unloaded the jet ski near the town of Branford, an older gentleman stood nearby leaning against his RV, watching us and asking questions. Will made some friendly small talk while securing the day's supplies onto the jet ski. Once they took off down the river, I stayed behind and introduced myself to the man. His name was Kevin, and he told me he was from Michigan.

"I was born in Michigan!" I said, lighting up.

Kevin and I chatted about Michigan for a while. I made a comment about how cold the weather could get early April—something like, "April showers bring snow plowers." We both laughed and admitted were glad to be in Florida. Kevin was super friendly and young at heart and always had something funny to say. He had been wanting to kayak down a smaller but more beautiful river nearby called the Santa Fe. It sounded intriguing, so we came up with a brilliant plan. We would load our kayaks into Kevin's RV, drive upstream, put in on the Santa Fe, and paddle back down to where the truck was parked. From there, we would load the kayaks into the truck and return them to the RV. That way, we wouldn't have to paddle back upstream and could enjoy more of the day floating on the river.

Kevin and I were stoked. Soon we were driving down some old dirt road, trying to find a place to put the kayaks in the water and park the big vehicle. After finding a parking spot, we unloaded the boats and embarked on an enjoyable kayaking excursion down the Santa Fe River, which is a tributary river of the Suwannee. Drifting past numerous springs and exploring, we marveled at the vibrant blue hues of Ginnie Spring and the majestic trees draping over the river.

Along the way, Kevin talked about different things. He asked me about my background and my journey, providing an opportunity for me to share stories of my longboard trip and my faith in Jesus, as we paddled downstream. Our conversation meandered through topics of religion, politics, and philosophy, revealing Kevin's skeptical outlook on things. At one point, he said his life's mantra was "Don't believe anything you hear." Pausing to reflect, I playfully responded, "Should I believe what I just heard you say?" The question left Kevin momentarily stumped, but soon we started to laugh and felt more connected.

While we were floating, I pulled out my phone to snap a picture of Kevin. "Smile, Kevin!" I said as I pointed the camera at him. With his paddle raised high, Kevin struck a pose, exuding a lively smile on his face that perfectly captured his charisma and the joy of our kayak excursion. This moment was special to me because it reminds me that meaningful connections often begin with a simple conversation.

Following our adventure, we connected on Facebook, which kept us in touch for the next two years. Kevin described the day as "absolutely awesome." Reflecting on that encounter fills me with gratitude, but it sadly marked the final time I would ever see Kevin.

In December of 2020, Kevin sent me a message saying that he had pancreatic cancer and was given six months to live. I responded with a message of prayer for healing, and then Kevin sent me a thumbs-up. Though I never received a direct reply, I fervently hoped for his recovery. Years passed before I messaged Kevin again, only to discover that he passed away in 2021, about seven months after his initial prognosis. The memory of Kevin's spirit and the profound connection we shared endure as a good reminder of life's fragility and the enduring power of human connection. In his honor, I wrote him this poem:

"The Blue Santa Fe"

(In Memory of Kevin Majeski)

A story of sorrow, quiet and deep, left me a treasure my soul will keep.

The paths that we wandered never told us the plan, just a word to begin it and a shake of the hand.

We floated together where cool waters lay, drifting down veins of the blue Santa Fe.

A radiant smile on my friend's tan face, at home once again in his happiest place.

I heard all his jokes and enjoyed every laugh, not thinking his life would be so quick to pass.

I wished again to see him someday, though we never crossed paths on the blue Santa Fe.

I know that one day we'll meet over there. We'll float crystal rivers and breathe in the air.

Basking in beauty, bathing in light, taking in scenes of eternal delight.

It's only a moment till we meet on that Day and remember our time on the blue Santa Fe.

After Kevin and I made it back to our vehicles, we said our final goodbyes. I checked my phone and saw a message from Will—they were nearing the Gulf Coast. We agreed to meet at a boat launch in Suwannee, Florida. I climbed into the truck and headed that way, and before long, they arrived at the river delta, where the freshwater of the Suwannee merged with the salt water of the sea.

To celebrate the moment, Will let me take the jet ski out for a quick ride. I eased into the delta with a mix of caution and excitement, then pushed out into the open waters of the ocean. The breeze, the sunlight, the vastness of the ocean, it was all surreal. I snapped a quick photo to capture it. After a short ten-minute cruise, I returned to the boat launch, where Will already had the trailer waiting.

The ride back to Mississippi took about seven hours. The truck easily covered the distance in one night, what took me weeks on a longboard. We pulled into Will's place well past 1 a.m., exhausted but satisfied. The trip had been a huge success for Will and Juliana, a one-of-a-kind adventure down the iconic Florida river.

For me, the longboard journey was never just about skating across America. It was about moments like these. I met people I never would have met, shared in their lives, and said yes to the unexpected. Whether I was riding a board or a jet ski, sleeping under the stars or getting handed the keys to a truck by a near-stranger, it was all part of something bigger. This trip was about connection, about faith, and about experiencing life in ways I never could have planned.

The next day, I was feeling like it was time for me to continue on the longboard trip, but I was about a hundred miles from my next host in New Orleans, Louisiana. Exactly 53 miles from the state border and another 47 miles to NOLA (New Orleans, Louisiana). Will wanted to help me any way that he could, so first he bought me my second pair of shoes, which I very much appreciated. Then we came up with a plan that allowed me to break up that 100-mile day of longboarding into two 50-mile days.

Early one morning, Will dropped me off where he had originally picked me up the first day we met. From there, I longboarded along the Biloxi coast through Gulfport and over the Bay St. Louis Bridge. I enjoyed the beautiful scenery of the blue ocean and white sandy beaches along the way. When I got to the intersection of Highway 90 and 607, nearing the Mississippi–Louisiana border, Will was there to pick me up with his truck. He took me back to his place and hosted me another couple of nights, so I could regain my strength. In the morning, he drove me back to the same location so that I didn't miss a single mile on the longboard. It was super convenient.

"You sure you don't want me to drive you down Highway 90 to the Louisiana border?" Will asked.

"Nope!" I responded. "If I wanted to take a vehicle across America, I wouldn't have sold mine back in Miami."

"Well, what if I pulled you to the border with my truck?" Will suggested, "It's only about seven miles from here. There's not much traffic down this road and probably no cops."

I paused for a second, considering his proposal, then replied, "Yeah, why not? That sounds like a lot of fun!"

So, Will rolled down his window and drove about thirty miles an hour as I held onto the back of his truck for dear life. It was an exhilarating rush, clinging to the truck with both hands. I was a bit nervous, but Will was so confident in my abilities that he swiftly cruised down the road, and we made it to the bridge in no time.

After Will got out of the truck, I looked at him and said, "I guess this is it, huh?"

I suddenly felt sad because Will, Juliana, Aubrey, and I had become so close and experienced so much together in the past six weeks. I had already said goodbye to the girls the day before as they were leaving to go to their mom's house, but now I had to say goodbye to Captain Will.

"Ah, this ain't the end, Daniel," Will said. "It's only the beginning. We will see you again. And just know that you always have a place to stay in Mississippi. You have my number, so don't hesitate to call if you ever need anything."

"OK," I responded. "Thank you for everything, Will. You've become a great friend, and I won't forget you." I reached out and gave Will a hug.

"We won't forget you either, Daniel. You've made a great impact here, and we've all loved being around you. So, this isn't goodbye but until next time."

"OK then," I responded with a smile and repeated, "Until next time."

With that, I turned around and jumped on my board. Will got back in his truck and headed home. I watched Will drive away and waved from a distance as we both went our separate ways. As I coasted on my longboard toward the bridge leading into Louisiana, memories of my time in Mississippi flooded my mind. Honestly, I hadn't expected to stay as long as I did; it was over six weeks. I could feel the days growing longer and hotter during my stay at Will's place in Biloxi.

As I approached Louisiana, I realized how much I had underestimated Mississippi. I assumed it would be plain and uneventful, yet six weeks of adventure changed my perspective completely. This state became one of the most impactful parts of my journey, thanks largely to Captain Will. He showed me how to face each day with positivity, to look for solutions rather than dwell on problems, and to create memories that last. In the end, Will and his daughters gave me more than a place to stay. They showed me that every place holds hidden adventures if you just learn to look.

These lessons have stayed with me, shaping the rest of my journey and instilling a sense of hope and confidence in persevering. On May 1, 2018, I crossed over the Pearl River, snapped a picture next to the Louisiana welcome sign, and felt a renewed determination to keep going.

CHAPTER 7.

STOPPED BY COPS

MAY 1, 2018 – MAY 22, 2019

NEW ORLEANS, LOUISIANA TO THE WOODLANDS, TEXAS

I used to imagine that obstacles meant I should stop, but now I believe they're meant to make us better.

Almost a whole year had passed since I crossed the Pearl River into Louisiana. It was now March of 2019, but I hadn't gone any further than Baton Rouge, Louisiana. I still had two-thirds of the state left to cross. So, what was taking me so long? Had I been arrested and sent to jail?

After crossing into Louisiana in 2018, I snapped a picture next to the welcome sign and then longboarded to Nate and Krista Peavy's home just north of downtown New Orleans. I'd met them during a trip to NOLA back in 2015, and they had become great friends of mine and still are to this day. They kindly welcomed me back, and we caught up over some delicious Jambalaya that Krista had cooked up. They told me I could stay with them for as long as I wanted, which made me feel right at home.

By this point, I had traveled roughly a thousand miles from Miami to New Orleans, spending nearly five months on the road from January 18 to May 5, 2018. With the summer heat starting to rise in Louisiana, I took time to reflect and pray and eventually made the decision to pause the journey. I wanted to take a break, so Krista dropped me off at the New Orleans airport, and I caught a flight back to Greenville, South Carolina.

The plan was simple: I would work through the summer, save money, and buy the gear I wanted to finish the longboard trip strong. But as it turned out, the summer had plans of its own. It started by me attending a weekly worship night at a place called The Jesus Warehouse. The first night I showed up, I was baptized by four men who became close friends: Jesse

Kinnunen, Evan Adams, Jed Aho, and Weyman Dodson. I had been baptized as a child, but I didn't start following Jesus until I was nineteen years old, and I had the feeling that I should be baptized again.

From there, things took off. I joined The Jesus Warehouse on a mission trip to New Hampshire. I also went to the Newport Folk Music Festival in Rhode Island with my friend Colton because he had a free ticket. And toward the end of the summer, I traveled to the country of Norway for another ten-day mission trip with Weyman, Evan, Colton, and a few others. Needless to say, saving money didn't go quite as planned. By the end of the summer, I hadn't bought any new gear, and my bank account was just as empty as my longboard backpack. But spiritually, I had been filled in ways I never expected and learned so much from each person and experience.

At the end of the summer, I found myself at a crossroads. I needed to get serious about saving money for a few items: a new backpack and a phone to take better pictures on the longboard trip. On top of that, the place where I'd been staying in Greenville was about to become unavailable, and I didn't have a vehicle. I needed direction, so I asked God to step in and provide a way forward. Not long after, I went over to my friend Reece's house. We were just hanging out on his back porch next to his 2004 black-and-cream Harley-Davidson Sportster. It had a muscular V-twin engine, Vance & Hines pipes, and an unmistakable roar. I thought Reece was cool whenever he rode it, but then he surprised me by saying that he wanted to give it to me. He tossed me the keys and said, "It's yours."

"Are you serious, Bro?" I asked in amazement. "I've never even ridden a real motorcycle before," I told him. But he grinned and said, "Just ride it like you stole it!" Then he signed the title over to me.

With the Harley as my new ride, and the summer coming to an end, I began exploring new job options and reached out to my best friend, Tristan Poss, who was living up in Wisconsin. He and his dad, Doug, ran a home improvement business and said they could use my help. Tristan invited me to come work with them. I ended up spending the winter there, saving money, buying the items I needed for the trip, and preparing to go back and finish what I had started.

When spring arrived, I stored my motorcycle in a friend's garage, bought a bivy, and flew back to New Orleans to continue the longboard trip. A bivy is basically what you get when a tent and a sleeping bag become one. During the first thousand miles, I hadn't carried any sleeping gear because I felt God didn't want me to, but after taking a yearlong break, something in me shifted and I decided to bring one along. Looking back, I realize my faith in God's provision on the road wasn't as strong as it had been, but even then, He was gracious. He continued to provide so many hosts that I eventually mailed the bivy back home.

I returned to New Orleans on March 4, 2019, right in the middle of Mardi Gras. The party atmosphere was at its climax, and after a couple weeks with Nate, Krista, and their church friends, I continued west toward Baton Rouge. I camped along the way, crossed the Mississippi River on March 22, and filmed everything because I wanted to start a YouTube channel, which got me distracted from continuing westward.

After crossing the river, I called Krista to pick me up and take me back to NOLA. Once we got back to their house, I began spending my days at Starbucks, learning everything I could about editing, branding, and content strategy. Meanwhile, my sister Carol, who works for United Airlines, added me to her free flight benefits for the entire year of 2019. One spontaneous decision led to another, and when Notre Dame caught fire on April 15, I booked a flight to Paris and left a note on Nate and Krista's counter, letting them know that by the time they read it, I'd already be on my way to France. They were so shocked when they woke up and read my note; we still laugh about this to this day. On my return, I stopped in Nebraska to visit family, then flew to South Carolina to see some friends.

The next few weeks were full of activity, but I lacked direction. I was chasing every exciting opportunity that came my way and losing sight of the longboard journey, but then I refocused. On May 15, I had Krista drop me back off at the exact spot she picked me up weeks before. I hadn't uploaded a single video on YouTube, but it was time to continue west.

I began longboarding down Lobdell Highway 415. I felt a mixture of emotions that day. Discouraged that I had taken so much time off in order to avoid the heat, I found myself back in Louisiana exactly a year later, right before the start of the summer. On the other hand, I was so excited to be getting on with this trip because I had dreamed of it every day since I had left, and now I could actually turn the dream back into actions. A new vigor came over me; I was determined to finish this trip if it was the last thing I ever did.

Lobdell Highway ran north into Highway 190. I took a left at the intersection and continued west. After riding about twenty-five miles down the Ronald Reagan Highway, I came to a long bridge that crossed the Atchafalaya National Wildlife

Refuge. Google Maps showed the bridge extending for about 6 1/2 miles (10 kilometers). There was no shoulder, only a small curb of concrete, enough for one person to barely walk on. I stopped for a second just staring at the long bridge in front of me, thinking about what to do as cars whizzed by. There was no other way that I knew of to keep going west, so it was either start walking across the long bridge or turn around.

Well, I wasn't gonna turn around, and I also wasn't going to ask anyone for a ride; that didn't even cross my mind. So, I kicked up my board, tucked it under my arm, and started walking along the edge of the bridge. But I walked on the left side of the bridge so that I could see the traffic coming toward me; I didn't want to get hit from behind. Once I made this decision, I was pretty much stuck on one side because there was a concrete divider in the middle of the four lanes that separated the two sides of traffic. Sometimes there wouldn't be any cars coming. When this happened, I would longboard on the road until I could see a vehicle in the distance. Then I would kick my board up and keep walking on the edge.

The bridge was flat and sat about twelve feet above the marsh below; it was completely flat as far as the eye could see. As I walked, sometimes my right foot would slip off the curb onto the white line that marked the boundaries of the road. It was only scary if there was a vehicle driving by when it happened. At some point, I paused to look over the thick concrete railing on my left as cars whizzed by on my right. I couldn't see much but swampy water and thick vegetation. I imagined that there was an alligator somewhere out there gazing at me; it looked like the exact place where an alligator would wait for its next meal. Suddenly, I was startled by a loud air horn. *"WAAHH!*

WAAHH!" A semi-truck driver was getting my attention to lean out of the way. On the truck's bumper was a banner that read OVERSIZED LOAD, and he was moving toward me at highway speed.

The driver blew his horn again. *"WAAAH WAAAH!"* He was getting closer to me, but he wasn't slowing down. The driver was transporting a mobile home that was taking up both lanes of traffic. Its side mirrors on the front of his truck extended even farther than the width of the house he was pulling. I had to lean way over the railing of the bridge to avoid getting hit in the face. *"WOOOOOSH!"* The wind blew in my ears. My face had barely missed the mirrors while the truck barreled by.

As I was hanging onto the railing with one hand and holding my longboard with the other, the alligators were hoping I would fall into the water. After the mobile home passed, I continued on with a little more pep in my step because I wanted to get off this bridge ASAP. I had already been on the bridge for an hour, and Google Maps showed that I wasn't even halfway across this massive thing. Between the heat of the sun and the stress of the cars whizzing by, I was exhausted, but I couldn't give up. Way off in the distance, I could see the bridge rising in elevation, which did give me some hope that things were changing soon. And I was right, things did change soon, really soon.

The next moment, I heard another alarming sound, *"whoop, whoop."* I recognized it right away. To my right were the blue-and-red lights flashing on top of a white SUV. It was the sheriff from the Louisiana Police Department on the other side of the concrete median. He had gotten out of his vehicle and was stopping all the traffic.

"Get over here!" he shouted, gesturing me over with one hand while signaling the traffic to stop with the other. I quickly walked across the two-lane highway and jumped over the concrete barrier. "Get in!" he demanded. I opened the back door to his SUV, set my board inside, climbed into the back seat, and closed the door. It was much quieter inside the vehicle, and there was AC, which felt great. I was bummed that I wasn't longboarding, but thankful that he was traveling in the same direction I had been going. I was trying to keep a positive attitude because I figured that he would eventually let me go. "Where are you going?" the sheriff asked in a calmer tone.

"I'm headed to San Francisco," I responded. He paused for a while to process what I had just said. "You shouldn't be out on this bridge. It's not for pedestrians because it's not safe," he stated.

"I'm sorry," I apologized. "I'm just trying to get across America, and I didn't know any other way to go through this area."

Although he didn't approve of what I had done, in the end, he dropped me off in Krotz Springs, at the other end of the bridge. I thanked him for keeping me safe and walked away. The ride was a lot more convenient than walking, but I was feeling disappointed because after longboarding over a thousand miles, I now had ridden a portion of the trip inside a vehicle. My pride wanted me to go back to the bridge and redo the missed miles, but I knew that was a bad idea.

I began to think more deeply about what it would mean to someday say, "I longboarded across America." Would I truthfully be able to claim this at the end of my trip? Did the car ride just discredit my achievement? I wasn't really sure, but then I thought about all the walking I had also done. Was I disqualified from "longboarding across the USA" because I didn't have my foot on the longboard for every inch of the trip due to the number of miles I had to walk? Then it hit me. I wasn't out there trying to set a Guinness World Record or anything. I was out here to enjoy longboarding and love people along the way. *It's not about you completing every single mile on this longboard,* I felt in my spirit. *It's about the people you'll meet along the way, the opportunities you'll have to impact them, and all the things you'll learn from that.*

I felt a lot more peace about this new perspective and began to shift the purpose of my journey toward connecting more with the people instead of worrying about how much pavement was rolling underneath my wheels. On the bright side, it was kinda nice to have traveled to Krotz Springs in just seven minutes when it would have taken me over an hour on my own. It was getting close to dinnertime, so I went and got something to eat from the general store nearby.

After dinner, I began looking for a place to set up my bivy. I tried to find a place that was secluded because I didn't want to have any more encounters with the police. I noticed that there was a nice, grassy area underneath the last section of the bridge. The spot was moderately secluded from the town, and it was dry, so I decided to set my tent up there.

The sun had gone down just as I finished setting up. With my headlamp on, I put everything inside the bivy and brushed my teeth. I also had a pack of baby wipes that I used to wipe down my body from the dirt and sweat. Trevor, who had walked across America, taught me this little trick. I then took out my journal and wrote about the things that happened that day before falling fast asleep.

Not long into my slumber, two bright beams of flashlight pierced through the darkness, jolting me awake. "Hey, what are you doing?" a man asked in an authoritative voice. I could tell it was another Louisiana police officer. Groaning, I unzipped my bivy and noticed two towering figures standing over me, their flashlights shining brightly into my face. Struggling to adjust to the sudden glare, I propped myself up on one arm and shielded my eyes with my hand. "I just set up my tent here. I'm traveling across the United States," I explained wearily.

With a more friendly tone, he said, "OK, well, we just wanted to check and see what was going on."

"Thanks, am I ok to be here?" I asked, still trying to wake up.

"Yep! You're good," he responded.

Then the other one said, "Nice tent! And are you going across on this board?" He pointed to my longboard, which was sitting outside my tent.

"Yeah," I said. It was pitch black outside, and they still had their lights on me, so I asked, "Do you want me to come out or something?"

"Oh no! You're good, man. Alright, have a safe trip."

"Thanks," I responded, and then they walked away. I was glad I didn't have to move, but I was startled by the experience. It had been the second cop encounter in the past twelve hours. I zipped my tent back up and gave a sigh of relief, knowing it was OK to sleep there. After a few more minutes, I calmed down and fell back asleep, until my alarm went off. "Beep, beep, beep!" It was 3 a.m., and although I was tired, I packed up my belongings and began longboarding west in the dark.

It was best to get a head-start before the sun came out with its scorching heat, but longboarding in the dark came with its challenges. On the one hand, the air was cool and felt refreshing, and the sun wouldn't drain my energy. On the other hand, I had to be careful because it was harder for me to see and harder for others to see me. The headlamp helped light my path, but there were always bits of gravel that would sometimes catch one of my wheels, stopping the board and causing me to fall forward. I usually would be able to catch myself and run through it, but there were maybe three times the whole trip that I tumbled on the pavement headfirst with my hands out to break the fall. The best perk of riding in the dark was being able to see the shining stars twinkling in the sky. They were always there drifting above me, and I loved watching them. I could look up at them and feel as if I didn't have any worries in the world.

For the next 8 days, I was covering an average of 30 miles (64 kilometers) a day and ended up sleeping in my tent anywhere I could find a place. I camped outside for seven nights in a row, which turned out to be the longest period of time that I would ever have to do that. Sometimes I slept under bridges, other times in the woods. There weren't any places to take showers, so I would just bathe in a lake or use my baby wipes.

During this week of camping, I met all kinds of people. I would pray about where I should stop to eat and rest, and God always seemed to bring strangers into my life who would ask me questions, and then we would end up hanging out for hours at a time. Sometimes they would even buy me a meal or show me around town. Tray and Zach were two high school students I hung out with one day. They began talking to me in McDonald's, and I could sense that they were searching for answers in life, so it was good that God brought our paths together. At the end of the day on May 16, I was thankful for the new friends I had made and continued westward.

The next day, at the 190 Truck Stop on the west side of Opelousas, Louisiana, I met Richard, an older and wiser man with much life experience. He ended up buying me a meal at McDonald's. He was full of quotable phrases like, "A smart man knows how to make money, and a wise man knows how to keep it." Richard and I kept in touch after we parted ways and would talk often on the phone. We've become pretty good friends, and we still talk to this day. Five years since we met at that truck stop, and we're still communicating. In fact, as I write this, he texted me:

> *Good morning, Dan, you're a true friend and a blessing to me. In life, there's some ups and downs. Knowing God's word, he will never leave you nor forsake you. That's what I have to hold on to. Please don't give up on me, keep praying for me. I learned a few things along the way, and one of them is: if someone loves you, you'll know it, and if someone doesn't, you'll know that too. I feel that you love me just like Christ would. That means more to me than I can say. The Bible says a friend sticks closer than a brother. You've proven that to me. I can tell that you're very happy. The Lord says it's not good for a man to be alone. Take care of yourself and your family. Rich.*

That night, after meeting Richard, I lay in my tent feeling grateful for all the people I was crossing paths with on this journey. I had pitched the tent in what I thought was a snug corner of the woods, perfect for a quiet night's sleep. As I drifted off, something brushed against the side of the tent. My first thought was that Florida's wildlife had finally come to claim me. The nudging continued, so I shouted and shook the tent like a lunatic, which didn't have much of an effect. Summoning courage, I unzipped the flap, switched on my headlamp, and prepared for the worst. Instead of a bear, or at least a deranged raccoon, I was confronted by a small, whitish-yellow armadillo. Startled by the light, it waddled off into the night. I was relieved, though embarrassed that a little armadillo had reduced me to acting like a frightened thirteen-year-old.

The next day, having survived another night in the wild, I was up early and on my way to Eunice, Louisiana. After a few hours of longboarding, the sun came up, and I was feeling a bit hungry. I stopped at McDonald's on Highway 190, where I met some friendly locals. When they learned about my journey across America, they were thrilled. Spontaneously, I decided to have them sign the back of my longboard with a permanent marker. A lady named Yvett was the first to leave her mark. From then on, everyone I met added their signature to my board, and it quickly became covered with names.

On May 20, 2019, I crossed the Sabine River on the Highway 12 bridge and officially entered Texas, which is less a state and more a landmass that could be its own country. I stopped to take my traditional photo by the welcome sign, feeling quite proud of the progress I had made. Louisiana had offered me no Couchsurfing hosts whatsoever, which was odd, though I did manage to cover more than 150 miles in 5 days. My next host was in The Woodlands, just north of Houston, my only friend between me and California. His name was Austin, a buddy from my college days in Wisconsin.

He was originally from Texas and had moved back to the suburb of Houston called The Woodlands after finishing college. Austin was a janitor for a megachurch in the area but ran a church of his own out of his house called the Abode Church. He and his wife, Anna, were incredibly kind-hearted and had graciously offered to host me whenever I reached their town. With an estimated two more days of travel ahead of me, I continued down the road, looking forward to connecting with them.

In Beaumont, Texas, I crossed the eight-lane Purple Heart Memorial Bridge over the Neches River on Interstate 10. From there, I followed a long stretch of road northwest on Route 105 toward The Woodlands, which was about as enjoyable as skating across a frying pan. The Texas sun hammered me like it had a personal grudge, the road was a patchwork of gravel and potholes, and my feet were about to resign after several hours of abuse. I was somewhere in the middle of nowhere, a good hour from the nearest gas station, and the only scenery to speak of was cars screaming by, close enough to trim my hair.

Just as I was praying that God would keep me alive, I heard a familiar sound from behind me: "whoop, whoop." Another police officer was trying to get my attention. I turned and saw the red-and-blue lights flashing on the windshield and the grill of his black SUV. This time it was the Liberty County Police. I stopped riding and watched as two officers stepped out of their vehicle and began walking toward me across the broiling asphalt.

In a very friendly tone, the taller officer began, "Hey man! What are you doing out here?"

"I'm headed to California."

"Dude! That's awesome," he responded. Then he asked where I was coming from.

"Miami, Florida," I said.

"Dang! That's far away from here. And you've been ridin' this board the whole way?" he asked with a bit of a Texas twang in his voice.

"Yep!"

"Well, we got a call about a guy skateboarding down the road, so we had to come see what was up."

"Am I doing anything illegal?" I asked.

"No, it's perfectly legal for you to be out here, although this road is very dangerous because people tend to drive so fast and aren't looking for pedestrians. If you want, we can give you a ride to town where the shoulder is wider and safer. It's about a seven-minute drive."

I had never voluntarily accepted a ride before, but something about this moment made me feel like I should. Maybe God was protecting me from some danger on this road by sending these cops to help me, so I accepted their offer.

Before we left, I asked, "Do you mind if I get a picture with you guys?"

"Sure thing, dude! And I want one with you too," one officer said.

So, we all took the pictures we wanted right there on the side of the highway and then got in their SUV and continued west. They asked all about me and my trip so far, and I got to know them a little bit too. That short drive shaved off about an hour on the longboard, and they dropped me off at a nice Shell gas station called Fuel Maxx 46, where the road was newer and much safer. It was at the intersection of route 105 and 2581 between the towns of Franklin and Cleveland, Texas. I had the officers sign the back of my board, which they thought was so cool, and then I asked if I could pray for them. They accepted, and I prayed a short prayer of protection, peace, and blessing over them. Then we waved goodbye, and I continued on to The Woodlands.

During my trip, I ran into plenty of deterrents: the sweltering southern heat, a year-long break, rough gravel roads, bridges that went on forever, and more than a few encounters with the police. Life has a way of tossing obstacles in front of us like it's setting up an obstacle course, forcing us to stop and think. I used to imagine those interruptions meant I was on the wrong path, but I've learned challenges can be used to make us better. Each challenge helped me grow, refocus, and push forward. If I had given up, I would have missed the best parts waiting just beyond the struggle, like seeing my story on the evening news. Good things come to those who keep going.

CHAPTER 8.

I'M ON TEXAS TV?

MAY 22 – JUNE 7, 2019
THE WOODLANDS TO GOLDTHWAITE, TEXAS

I used to imagine that recognition was just about fame, but now I believe it can open doors to an abundance of new connections.

After riding more than 300 miles on my longboard and camping by the roadside for seven nights, I finally rolled into Conroe, just north of The Woodlands, Texas, on May 22, 2019. Austin's wife, Anna, met me at a Shell gas station where Highway 105 meets North Loop 336 and drove me to their house. There I was introduced to their housemate, Tanner, who rented a room from them. The two highlights of the day were meeting new friends and taking my first shower in seven days. Never in my life had hot water and soap felt so glorious.

When Austin arrived home from work, we all hung out together. It turned into one of those evenings where the conversation comes easy and the laughter even easier. I enjoyed getting to know Tanner and Anna and catching up with Austin; it felt like time well spent. The next day, Austin kindly joined me for a trip to REI to exchange my air mattress, which had inconveniently given up on me during the week of camping. REI replaced it at no cost. Between reconnecting with Austin and his hospitality, and walking out of REI with a brand-new mattress, my short visit felt rich with good things.

On May 25, Austin dropped me off at the same gas station where Anna had first picked me up, and I pushed west once again. After about twenty miles, I rolled into Montgomery, Texas, and spotted a small donut shop called Shipley Do-Nuts. The smell was enough to make me float inside. I ordered a donut, and only after the man behind the counter had plucked it from the case did I discover they only accepted cash. I didn't have a dime. Embarrassed, I stood there watching as he slid the donut back onto the rack beneath the glass case, while in my head, I was screaming, *Nooo, please.* Just then, the man behind me in line said, "Hey man, I'll buy it for you."

"Really?" I responded. While in my head, I was thinking, *Thank God, I just about lost a donut and my dignity.*

"Yeah man! It's no problem!" Then he ordered what he wanted, took out his wallet, and paid for everything. "It looks like you're on a journey," he continued. "Where are you going?"

"I'm going to San Francisco."

"On that board?" he asked with a surprised tone.

"Yep!"

He thought that what I was doing was incredible, so he was glad to meet me. His name was Russel, and he asked me if I had ever tried a kolache.

"No. What's that?" I asked.

"Oh man, you can't go longboarding through Montgomery, Texas, without trying a kolache!" Russel exclaimed. "It's basically like a hot bun with a sausage inside. Here, let me buy you one so you can try it."

Russel ordered me a kolache, paid for it, and handed it to me.

"You know," Russel told me, "Montgomery was the birthplace of the Texas State flag." We chatted a bit more before he said, "Well, I gotta get going to work, but it was great to meet you, Daniel."

I shook Russel's hand, thanked him, and then he took off in his truck. I pulled the donut and kolache out of the paper bag and began eating them both. Right as I was taking the last bite of my kolache, Russel whipped his truck back into the parking lot, got out, started walking toward me, and said, "Hey, I totally forgot to ask, but do you want something to drink?"

I was indeed feeling thirsty, so I said, "Dude, that would be great!"

We went back into Shipley's, and Russel bought me two blue Powerades. I was super thankful for that kind gesture and was so surprised that he had come back just to buy me a drink. I had him sign the back of my board and then prayed a blessing over him. Then he left for good, and after I finished one of my Powerades, I did too.

The encounter with Russel lifted my spirits so much that riding suddenly felt easy. The road helped too, freshly paved and smooth enough that I could actually enjoy some speed without rattling my bones to pieces. Any time I hit a stretch like that, it felt like rolling on air. After about twenty miles, I reached the town of Navasota. Longboarding down its main street was like stepping back in time. The old western architecture made me half expect a cowboy to ride out of a saloon and challenge me to a duel, longboard versus horse.

When I reached the edge of town, I ducked into the DG Market and picked up a pack of thank-you cards. Then I found a picnic table in a small park by Cedar Creek, sat down, and began writing notes to the people who had helped me along the way. I dropped them off at the local post office before moving on. I like to think that free kolache set something in motion, inspiring kindness that stretched beyond me. Russel surely never imagined his small gesture would find its way into a book and be read around the world. It reminded me that no act of compassion is ever too small, not even a single kolache freely given to a stranger.

Continuing west on Highway 105 for most of the day, I eventually turned right onto State Highway 6 and headed northwest toward College Station and Bryan, Texas. That night, I camped under a bridge by the Navasota River, about twenty miles from where my next Couchsurfing host lived. The spot was quiet, tucked beside the river with tall bushes, sandy ground, and just enough cover to feel hidden. It was dry, dark, and, best of all, free of police. I avoided sleeping directly beneath the bridge. The grass over there was tall, and I wasn't eager to share my bivy with snakes or anything else that slithered.

Exhausted, I crawled into my bivy, set my alarm for sunrise, and passed out almost instantly. When it went off, I rolled out, grabbed my phone, and filmed a quick video to show where I had slept. Watching it back, I noticed something unsettling. My face looked like it had lost an argument with a beehive. My cheeks, nose, and eyelids were puffed up in a way they had never been before. I blamed the pollen, shrugged, and pressed on. By mid-morning, the swelling was gone, and thankfully it never returned.

It took a few hours to ride to Bryan, Texas, which is just north of College Station. Chris, an alumnus of Texas A&M, graciously agreed to host me for three nights. Upon arrival, Chris provided me with a private bedroom and bathroom. After freshening up, we explored Texas A&M on bikes, visiting landmarks like the football field and the Lawrence Sullivan Ross statue. That evening, we dined at Layne's Chicken Fingers near campus, enjoying good food and conversation.

The next morning, May 26, I joined Chris in his garden before lunch, lending a hand with yard work and planting cucumber seeds. It was a laid-back day, much needed after a week of extensive longboarding, covering 150 miles since Beaumont and 1,500 miles (over 2,400 kilometers) since starting in Miami. Now I was nearing the halfway mark of my journey, and I felt a surge of excitement and confidence. The following day was Memorial Day; Chris and I spent it playing disc golf and swimming at his friend's pool. We enjoyed a delicious curry dinner before winding down with heartfelt conversations about travel, movies, music, and life. Little did I know Chris would be my final Couchsurfing host through the rest of the state. Bryan, Texas, left a lasting impression on me as it concluded another great Couchsurfing experience.

At 3:30 the next morning, I began my day with prayer and Scripture reading before quietly leaving Chris's home at 4:30 to resume my journey. I had said my goodbyes the night before and walked out of the house quietly. After covering 20 miles (32 kilometers), I stopped at a McDonald's in Hearne, where a man named John noticed my gear and struck up a conversation. I had left my longboard leaning against the outside wall near the entrance, like I always did. When we sat down with our food, he glanced out the window and asked, "You're not worried someone's gonna walk off with your board?"

I shook my head. "Nah. I've been doing that since Florida, and it's always there when I come back."

He smiled and said, "Well, I guess the Lord's watching over more than just you."

Learning about my trip, he kindly paid for my breakfast, and we talked about Jesus, Mormons, and baptism. The rich conversations I had with kind strangers I met along the road made me truly grateful. After John left, I began to ponder my next route. Having prayed for guidance over the last few days,

I considered my options—continue north toward Waco or head southwest toward Round Rock. I was aiming to stay on main highways and avoid interstates for a smoother journey to California, so Round Rock seemed like the better choice, but I still wasn't confident.

Before I left McDonald's, I got a text from an old friend from Wisconsin named Reid. He knew about my trip and felt moved to reach out and see how I was doing. It turned out he and his wife, Victoria, lived in Cedar Park near Round Rock. He offered to host me if I came through their area. What an answer to my prayer! I decided I would head their way after leaving McDonald's.

Before leaving, I checked a few social media notifications and noticed a comment from my great-uncle Jerry. He suggested I reach out to some news stations and tell them what I was doing so they could put my story on TV. The idea made me uneasy; it felt too much like self-promotion, and I wanted no part of that. I had always believed it was better to let another man praise your works and not your own mouth, just as Proverbs 27:2 says. So, I prayed, *If You want me on TV, Lord, You'll have to be the one to make it happen*. My job was to keep pushing toward the Pacific Ocean.

Heading toward Cedar Park, I had just turned left onto Highway 190 when my phone rang. It was Kim Metzler. She said an old college friend of hers named Jenny lived in Texas and might be somewhere along my route. If I passed through her town, I should reach out. Jenny had worked at a TV station in Texas and loved what I was doing. Kim asked if she could share my number. I told her that was fine and kept rolling, curious where this might lead.

About ten miles down the road, I stopped at a little grocery store in the small town of Gause. As I walked up to the front door of Coats Groceries, there was a lady sitting on the bench who asked, "Were you the guy that I passed on the road like five miles back riding that skateboard?"

"Yeah!" I responded.

"Well, why are you doing this?" she asked me. It was a frequent question inquisitive people asked.

"I'm longboarding across America in Jesus's name and sharing His love with those I encounter along the way."

"Wow!" she exclaimed.

Then the lady ushered me inside and announced to the other women in the store, "This gentleman is skateboarding across America and spreading the gospel as he goes."

One of the women stepped forward, held out her hand, and said, "I'm Paula. Can I buy you a cold drink?" She then introduced me to her granddaughter. "Here, can I get a picture of you with her?" she asked. After the snapshot, Paula took my hand and offered a heartfelt prayer. Touched by her kindness, I was further surprised when she pulled out $50 from her purse and handed it to me.

"Thank you so much," I said. "This is such a blessing."

"Where to next?" Paula inquired.

"I have a friend in Cedar Park, so I am heading there."

"It's too bad it's not Wednesday night; you could have spoken to our youth group." Her words and generosity left me humbled. It was a good reminder of the impact my journey was having on those I met along the way.

When I got back on the road, I pulled out my phone and recorded a short video about what had just happened. When

I looked up, a magnificent rainbow stretched across the sky behind me, following along as if the clouds and I were keeping the same pace. I still had no place to sleep, so I asked God to provide a safe and dry spot for the night. A couple of hours later, I found one tucked between the road and a set of train tracks that ran alongside it. I set up my bivy, cleaned myself with wipes, brushed my teeth, wrote in my journal, and drifted off to sleep.

As I slept, I slipped into a vivid dream as if watching a movie. My little tent was plopped squarely on the train tracks, with me tucked inside like some human burrito. A whistle shrieked in the distance, "Woooooo wooo!" My chest tightened as the deep roar of the engine and the clatter of iron wheels grew louder and louder. I tried to scramble out before it turned me into scrambled eggs, but my body felt glued to the ground. I even tried to open my eyes, but they refused to budge.

The whistle blasted again, a piercing "WOOOO WHOO!" that nearly ruptured my eardrums. I shot upright in my tent, gasping for air, as a real train thundered past on the tracks beside me. My heart tried to escape through my throat, sweat streamed down my face, and for a moment, I was certain this was the end of the line. But once the rails quieted and my pulse slowed, exhaustion dragged me back to sleep.

The next morning, as the sun was dawning, I got up and packed my tent; I could feel the humidity already building in the air. I grabbed my water bottle and drank the last bit. There was nothing but fields and trees around and nowhere to get anything to drink, and I was parched. I had forty miles to go before arriving at Reid and Victoria's apartment, and my feet were sore from the rough roads. It was not a pleasant ride, but I did my best to stay positive.

I made a video saying, "Good morning! Let's go! This is the day that the Lord has made, I *will* rejoice and be glad. It doesn't say, I *might*. It says, I *will* rejoice and be glad!" I was trying to encourage myself as this was the type of attitude I wanted to have every day, even when it was hot and I had no more water. After a long day of riding, and finally getting some water, I arrived at Reid and Victoria's apartment. It was so good to see friendly and familiar faces. I took a shower and headed to dinner in Austin with Reid.

The next day, I spent some time with God and began looking at the map, asking Him which way I should go. I felt like I should go north to Killeen, but I wasn't sure. Then my phone rang. It was Jenny, Kim's friend. Jenny was so excited to talk with me, and she was wondering if I would be traveling through Killeen. "Well," I said, "I was just asking God where I should go, so I guess I'll try Killeen."

"That's great!" Jenny said enthusiastically. "I used to work for the local TV station here in Killeen for twenty-five years. Would you be willing to be interviewed on TV?" she asked. "I know all the media people in town, and I'm sure they'd love to do a story."

I couldn't believe what I was hearing. Just two days ago, I had told God if He wanted me on the TV, He would have to arrange it. And now it was happening!

"So, when do you plan to arrive?" Jenny inquired.

"I plan to leave early tomorrow morning."

"You're welcome to stay with my husband and me," she said.

"That would be great!" I replied.

"OK. Are you sure you'll be alright? Do you want me to come pick you up or anything?"

"Nope. I'll be alright. Thanks for the offer, though," I responded.

Jenny was like me—always excited for an adventure.

"Well, I'll see you tomorrow then, honey. Just keep me in the loop."

"Thanks, Jenny! I will."

After I hung up, a couple of friends from Wisconsin happened to be nearby and offered to take me out for lunch. Stefanie and Claire picked me up, treated me to a meal, and then dropped me back off at Reid and Victoria's apartment. It was a short visit, but their generosity and encouragement meant a lot. I am still grateful for that simple act of kindness and the boost it gave me to keep pushing forward.

After lunch, I checked the weather report and saw that it was nice and clear, but only until five the next morning, when a big thunderstorm was predicted to hit Cedar Park. Reid had warned me that one was coming. Then I saw that the forecast was showing more thunderstorms during the next few days. There was no way I could longboard in weather like that, but I didn't want to get stuck in Cedar Park. I wanted to keep going! Then the thought came to my mind to leave for Killeen immediately.

As I contemplated the thought, I got a phone call from an unknown number; it turned out to be a reporter for KXXV, the ABC affiliate in Killeen. The reporter, Hunter Davis, asked me about my trip so far and wanted to do my story on camera. I was shocked! Not just because I might soon be on TV but because I never asked for it. I believe God heard my prayer and responded with, "OK, I'll do it!"

"So, when will you arrive?" Hunter asked.

"Umm, I think I'm gonna head there tonight."

"You're going to longboard to Killeen in the dark?" she asked with excitement and a bit of concern in her voice. "How far away are you?"

"I'm a little over fifty miles south of Killeen, just outside Round Rock. I have to leave tonight or else I will possibly get stuck here for the rest of the week because there is a big storm coming."

"Well, that sounds daring! Are you sure you should longboard in the dark?"

"I have a headlamp, so I'll be fine. But I gotta leave soon so I can beat this storm."

"OK, well, be safe and let me know when you get here. Then you can rest up, and we can come to the house where you're staying and do the interview there."

After we hung up, I was determined to go because I had just discussed my plans with the news reporter. I called Jenny and told her that I was on my way and expected to be there around 2 a.m. She was concerned, but I reassured her that I would be fine and that I didn't want to get stuck in this storm. She prayed with me for my safety.

At 8 p.m., I left Reid and Victoria's cozy apartment and ventured into the night. It was gusty and chilly, and the mist threatened rain. Doubts crept into my mind, so I asked God for clear skies. Miraculously, the rain clouds dispersed, revealing a vast expanse of stars in the heavens as I journeyed away from the city's glow. My headlamp was the only beacon of light illuminating my path. Crossing over the San Gabriel River, I gazed up at the Texas sky, noticing one star that was brighter than the rest, reminding me of the boundless beauty of the Lone Star State.

After four hours and thirty-two miles, I rolled into Florence, Texas at midnight. The shoulder on Highway 195 had been so rough that I bailed off the bypass, hoping the town streets would be smoother. They were, at least until a pair of headlights came barreling toward me. For a moment, I braced for another run-in with the cops, but it turned out to be two guys in a big truck, hollering something unintelligible as they roared past. Small-town entertainment, I guess. Once they sped off, I kept riding.

Soon enough, I was back on the bypass, and the moment my wheels touched Highway 195, I regretted it. The road was brutal. The pavement rattled through my board into my feet until my whole lower body went numb. Loose gravel sprinkled across the shoulder like landmines, stopping my board cold and sending me sprinting to avoid a faceplant. It was miserable, but I pushed on.

By 2 a.m., I reached the tiny town of Ding Dong. The name alone made me grin, though I should have been in Killeen by then. Lack of sleep pounded in my head, and the nine miles still ahead of me might as well have been ninety. At the intersection of 195 and State Route 2670, I spotted the Country Pride Market and saw an alternate route on the map. It added miles, but maybe the pavement would be better. I turned left, figuring Ding Dong was as good a place as any to change course.

For a few blissful minutes, it paid off. The road was smoother, I picked up speed, and the night air felt almost refreshing. My optimism lasted until I turned onto Maxdale

Road, where the pavement was worse than 195. My heart sank—eight miles to go, and now I didn't want to turn back. I trudged forward, and the road grew rougher still until it gave up altogether and became straight gravel. That was discouraging enough, but then a massive sign loomed out of the dark: NOTICE Now Entering Fort Hood Military Installation By entering this installation you consent to the search of your person and vehicle.

Perfect. I thought. *Not only am I exhausted, but now I'm probably trespassing on an army base.* I wanted to curl up in the ditch and sleep forever. Instead, I whispered a prayer for help and admitted the truth: Leaving Highway 195 in Ding Dong had been, quite literally, a ding-dong decision.

Around 3:15 a.m., headlights appeared behind me and a vehicle slowed down. My first thought was that I was about to be hauled off by the U.S. military for being somewhere I clearly didn't belong. To my relief, it was just a friendly guy on his way to an early morning shift at work who pulled over and offered me a ride. I didn't hesitate. I was about to fall over from exhaustion, and besides, a longboard is no match for gravel. Once inside, he explained that the army used that land to train infantry and tanks. "Well, I'm glad you picked me up, then," I said with a weary sigh. I was deeply grateful he rescued me, not only from a possible run-in with soldiers but also from collapsing in the ditch from sheer lack of sleep.

After fifteen minutes, the road smoothed out, and I asked him to stop. I thanked him for the ride, stepped out, and longboarded over to the Wal-Mart on the Schlueter Loop. As I rolled along, I called Jenny. "Oh, I'm so glad you are safe," she said. "I didn't sleep at all tonight because I was so worried about you." It was now 4 a.m., and I was two hours behind thanks to some rough circumstances and one bad decision. Still, I had finally made it to Killeen, and that was worth celebrating.

In no time at all, Jeff and Jenny pulled up in their black sedan and greeted me warmly with a hug. Our bond was strong from the start. On the way to their house, I told them how I took a wrong turn in Ding Dong and found myself on Fort Hood's reservation land. "Oh my!" Jenny exclaimed, "You could have stepped on a landmine! I can't believe you got lost in Ding Dong, Texas! That's hilarious!"

When we reached their house, Jenny showed me the room I would be staying in, and Jeff left for work. I took a shower and then drank some fresh orange juice Jenny made for me. When I lay down in bed, I spotted a picture of Kim Metzler and her family on the nightstand beside me. It was good to know that I was in the house of a mutual friend. Then I fell fast asleep.

When I woke up a few hours later, on Thursday, May 30, I read a note from Jenny:

> Daniel, I will be home by 11:30 or 12:00. ABC-KXXV will call you. Help yourself to anything you need to eat, TV, etc. Jeff wants to take us all out to eat at Roadhouse tonight. I will take you around when I get back. :)

The reporter called to say she would be there by 12:30.

Jenny arrived home just before Hunter did. Through the window, we could see her van with the decal Central Texas News Now – 25 ABC on the side. Just before Jenny and I walked out the door, I asked God to give me the best words to say. Hunter was super friendly and easy to talk with. The interview lasted about forty-five minutes, and she let me hold her expensive video camera as I longboarded down the road recording my wheels and taking a video selfie. It was the first TV interview of my life, and I was super excited. When we finished, Hunter told me that my story would be featured on the six o'clock news, in four hours. Then she packed everything up and said goodbye.

"Alright, you ready to go into town?" Jenny asked.

"Where are we going?"

"I'm taking you over to the *Killeen Daily Herald.* You're gonna be in Friday morning's newspaper."

I couldn't believe that all of this was happening. That afternoon, I watched my story on the TV with Jenny in her living room, and the next morning, I was on the top of the front page of the *Killeen Daily Herald* with the full story inside. I had never seen myself on the TV or in a newspaper before, but there I was. Both news stories reported that I was "longboarding across the United States in the name of Jesus Christ, sharing His love with the people I met along the way."

That night, Jeff took us out to Texas Roadhouse for dinner. Over baskets of rolls and plates of steak, Jenny kept telling everyone that I had just been on TV and that I was longboarding across America. People actually wanted to take pictures with me, and I even had them sign the back of my board. For a moment, I felt like a celebrity, with Jenny proudly leading the fan club.

I stayed the weekend with Jenny and Jeff, then early Monday morning, June 3, 2019, Jenny dropped me off at the familiar Wal-Mart before dawn. After a quick goodbye hug, I set out for Lampasas, the next town on my journey. While I was en route, Jenny contacted the local newspaper there and arranged for them to reach out to me. I had no idea at the time, but that bit of media attention would open the door to new friendships and plenty of places to stay.

While boarding along the road to Lampasas, I came upon a guy walking along the shoulder of the highway. When I came up to him, I picked up my board and started walking. "Hello," I said, "I'm Daniel. What's your name?"

"Martin," he responded.

This Martin was much different than the first one I had met. He turned out to be refreshingly ordinary. As we walked together, Martin shared a bit about himself, and while we were talking, the local Lampasas newspaper called to schedule an interview with me for later that afternoon. Before the interview, Martin and I grabbed lunch at a small Mexican restaurant in town. It was simple but good, and by then, it already felt like Martin and I had known each other longer than the morning.

The interview was easygoing. We met the journalist in his office, and he asked me about my trip, my board, and why I was doing it. Martin came along and, to my surprise, slipped right into the role of unofficial publicist. It made me smile. He seemed proud to be the first person in Lampasas to meet me, and he even double-checked that they spelled his name correctly. The whole thing was lighthearted and fun, and I genuinely enjoyed his enthusiasm.

Afterward, Martin treated me to some ice cream, and then we made our way across town to a mission house where dinner was being served. On the way, we ran into Daris and his family. They were curious and full of questions about the longboard trip, and before we parted ways, Daris gave me his number and offered me a place to stay if I needed it. We prayed together on the sidewalk, and then Martin and I continued on to the mission house, where I shared a meal with more locals and soaked in the kindness of another small Texas town.

After dinner, I called Daris. He told me his wife, Ashley, had seen me on the news, and he gave me his address. They graciously hosted me for the night, and the next morning, Ashley's friend Justin stopped in. We talked for a bit, and he invited me for breakfast at McDonald's. We had a great time, and he introduced me to his wife, Christy. They offered to host me for as long as needed, and I stayed with them for a few days. One evening, they hosted a BBQ with friends, which was a lot of fun.

Early the following morning, I left Justin and Christy's house on my longboard, heading for Goldthwaite; it was June 7. I hadn't planned on staying in Lampasas that long, but God's ways are greater than our ways, and He had more surprises for me ahead. I had no connections in Goldthwaite, nor did I have any idea where I would eat and sleep. When I arrived in town, I sat down on a bench outside the library and asked God to provide a place for me to sleep that night. A few moments later, a lady pulled up in a minivan to drop off some books at the library. She looked at me twice and then said, "Are you the guy that I saw on TV?"

"Yes ma'am, that's me," I responded.

"I wanna take you to see the mayor. Get in the van."

Without hesitation, I jumped into the lady's van, and we headed to see the mayor. She drove to McMahan Pharmacy, owned by Mike McMahan, the mayor of Goldthwaite, Texas.

The lady introduced us, and I had Mike and her sign my longboard. Mike humorously taught me to pronounce the name of the town. "It's 'Gol-th-wait.' You need a lisp to say it," he told me.

While at the pharmacy, I met several locals. Wayne Wallace, a kind gentleman who was waiting patiently for his prescription, offered to host me at his house. Other locals who had gathered around started offering their homes too, including the mayor. Soon, Madison, a reporter from the *Goldthwaite Eagle*, arrived to interview me and take photos for the newspaper. After the interview, I had my choice of lodging. I kind of wanted to stay at the mayor's house, but I chose Wayne's since he was the first to offer. I called him, and within ten minutes, he returned to the pharmacy to pick me up. I thanked God for providing me with a place to stay.

That evening, Wayne invited me to his family reunion. Despite being tired, I decided to join him. I met many of his relatives and enjoyed good food and conversation. To my surprise, they wanted me to come back the next day for the main event.

"I thought this was the main event," I said.

One of the ladies chimed in, "Baby, this ain't nothing. Tomorrow you're gonna eat brisket so good, you'll think Jesus cooked it Himself."

Everyone laughed, and I couldn't help but smile too. I didn't know what tomorrow would hold, but if it was anything like this evening, I knew I'd be in for something special. The garage-turned-kitchen was lined with over fifty first-place BBQ trophies, each one a testament to years of perfecting the craft. The smoky scent of slow-cooked meat filled the air; it was rich and mouth-watering. Plates were stacked high with ribs, brisket, pulled pork, and all the fixings: cornbread, slaw, baked beans. One of the ladies handed me a piece of brisket, and the moment I took a bite, I knew she wasn't exaggerating. It melted in my mouth, tender and packed with flavor. To this day, it's still the best BBQ I've ever had.

At the BBQ, were several people my age, and we hit it off quickly. They took me around town to see an old suspension bridge, and then someone suggested we go swimming at the tank. "Umm, what's a tank?" I asked, picturing some oversized fish aquarium. Everyone laughed at my ignorance, assuring me it was plenty big since one of the guys was bringing a jet ski. I soon learned that in Texas, a "tank" is simply a pond or small lake. We spent the afternoon swimming and zipping around on the jet ski, and it turned out to be a blast.

As the sun began to set, we packed up our belongings and headed home. Throughout the day, a pretty girl named Julie had gradually begun talking to me and asking me more questions. As we were leaving the lake, she asked me, "Do you want me to take you back to the house?"

"That'd be great," I replied.

On the way, she suggested, "Why don't we stop at Dairy Queen and go eat at the park?"

"Sounds good to me," I said.

After getting our food, we drove around the park looking for a place to stop. By this time, it was dark, and our headlights swept across another vehicle parked in the shadows. "Look at their steamed-up windows. They are probably gettin' it on," she said. Eventually, she found a dimly lit spot and parked. We started eating, but after her first bite, she said, "I'm not very hungry anymore." That's when it dawned on me that food might not have been her main interest. I was a little naïve. I'd had girlfriends before, and purity had not always been my strength, but after following Jesus, I had made it my aim to keep myself for my future wife. Some might call that prudish. She was attractive, and I had the same impulses as any man, but I knew God could give me strength to say no. I prayed silently, *Lord, please give me wisdom and self-control in this moment.*

"Julie," I said, "I think you are very nice and attractive. I've really enjoyed spending time with you and everyone today. I'm a Christian and don't want to take advantage of you or take anything from your future husband. I hope you can understand where I'm coming from." She seemed to appreciate my words, but after about five minutes, she took me back to Wayne's house. When I was getting ready for bed that night, I felt a deep sense of relief and gratitude. It wouldn't have been healthy or right for us to act on our impulses, and I thanked God for giving me the strength to resist.

Reflecting on the day, I am deeply grateful for the generosity of both God and the people I met. The unexpected encounters and unforgettable experiences remind me of the importance of living fully and embracing the moment.

The news coverage I received in Texas became a turning point in my journey; it opened doors I never imagined. After my story aired in Killeen, other outlets in nearby towns began reaching out to interview me. Much of this was thanks to Jenny, who made it her mission to call every local station along my route. I started jokingly calling her my publicist, and she happily owned the title. By the time I reached the West Coast, she had connected me with TV stations and newspapers across

Texas, New Mexico, Arizona, and California, lining up more than twenty interviews.

The exposure brought unexpected blessings. People began recognizing me from the news and would offer me money, food, or even a place to stay. Their kindness was so consistent that I never had to use my bivy again; I eventually mailed it home. I used to imagine that recognition was just about fame, but now I believe it can open doors to an abundance of new connections. Southern hospitality was alive and well, and I was experiencing it in abundance, at least until the bad news started coming.

CHAPTER 9.

THREE DEATHS IN THREE WEEKS

JUNE 11 – JULY 12, 2019

GOLDTHWAITE TO BROWNWOOD, TEXAS

I used to imagine that life was long and full of endless opportunities, but now I believe each day is a gift meant to be lived with purpose and love.

After staying with Wayne for four nights, it was time for me to leave Goldthwaite. We had gotten along great, but the road was calling again. So, on Tuesday, June 11, I was up at 5 a.m. to begin my 32-mile ride to Early, Texas. I wanted an early start to stay ahead of the Texas heat. Wayne got up with me and made breakfast, which I appreciated. He also brewed coffee like he did each morning, but I explained I didn't drink coffee on longboarding days to avoid cramps; that left Wayne with the bonus of an extra cup for himself.

After we said goodbye at about 6 a.m., the sun was coming up. I never got tired of watching the sunrise while longboarding. The Texas sunrise was always enchanting—bright pink and orange beams mixing with the blue sky made a beautiful combination. I loved breathing the crisp morning air and enjoying the countryside before the traffic picked up. The flat landscape was dotted with short trees. The open fields were clothed in the most wonderful wildflowers with all kinds of animals: cattle, goats, and horses grazing on the grass. Every now and then, I would ride alongside or cross over little creeks. Some of the roads outside of Goldthwaite were rough, forcing me to pick up my board and walk. There was a brief moment when I looked back at the vast country I had already covered; the view along with the realization of my achievement was awe-inspiring. As the sun soon rose farther into the morning sky, more cars began flying by.

About a quarter of the way to Early, a white vehicle stopped, and a blonde-haired lady rolled down her window and said, "Are you Daniel Herman?"

I was a bit shocked to hear my name. "Yes, ma'am," I said.

"That's so cool," she responded. "I saw you in an article this morning on Facebook. It's so great to see you out here, and I want to give you this." Then she handed me thirty dollars.

I couldn't believe it, so I asked her if I could take a quick video. Her name was Kelly. She was from Goldthwaite, but she worked at a hair salon in Brownwood, one town over from Early. She gave me her cell phone number and told me that I should stop by her salon whenever I got to Brownwood. Encounters like this were so encouraging. As she drove away, I just smiled and thanked God for this incredible trip that I was on and for the people I was meeting along the way.

Around 10 a.m., Jenny called to tell me about a lady at the Early Visitor Center who wanted to meet me. Jenny had called her to let her know who I was and that I was headed her way. I thanked Jenny for her initiative and continued west. About an hour later, another car stopped. This time it was the lady from the visitor center, Denise, and she was excited to see me. She offered me a Gatorade and a promise of some Early hospitality upon my arrival. With only an hour of longboarding left, I was excited to reach my destination.

Soon the road smoothed out, and Wayne texted to ask where I was. I told him I had just reached the Early Visitor Center. Inside, a lady named Cookie greeted me, and Denise handed me a goody bag filled with snacks and other fun items. Then she introduced me to two reporters, one from the local newspaper and the other from the radio station. It was my first radio interview, and both went well. Not long after, Wayne pulled up in his truck with water, Gatorade, bananas, and snacks for energy. I was so grateful he had driven more than thirty minutes just to bring me food. I gave him a big hug before he headed back to Goldthwaite.

After Wayne left, Denise said, "We're gonna take you out to La Botana Mexican Grill for lunch." When we walked in, she told the manager that I was longboarding across the country. He smiled, impressed, and said the restaurant would cover my meal. Blessings seemed to be piling up one after another. Cookie arrived with her wife, Tresta, and we all dug into guacamole and tacos, laughing and talking like old friends. Afterward, I got a picture with the staff before Denise whisked me off again. She had lined up a meeting with the mayor, another radio interview, a stop at the newspaper office, and even a tour of Early.

When I mentioned that Kelly had invited me to her salon, Denise drove me there. Kelly was thrilled to see me and introduced me to her colleagues. She had even ordered takeout for me. I explained we had just eaten at La Botana's, but she said I could keep the food for later. Then she offered to have one of her stylists cut my hair. By this point in my journey, my hair had grown close to my shoulders. I didn't want to cut my hair short because long hair seemed to fit the vibe of longboarding across America. Instead, one of the ladies at the salon gave my hair a little trim.

While I sat in the chair, Kelly handed me her phone with the Amazon app open and said, "Here, type into the search bar the kind of wheels you use, and I will buy you new ones. The ones on your longboard are looking pretty rough." She was right; I hadn't changed my wheels since New Orleans. I was so thankful for her generosity. As usual, I got a big group photo and had everyone at the salon sign my board before saying goodbye.

Denise's last stop on the grand tour of Early was a clubhouse perched on the edge of town with a view of the golf course. We stood there admiring the scenery when she asked, "So, where are you planning to spend the night?"

"Maybe at a campsite," I said. The truth was I had no idea, but I had learned not to admit that my real plan usually involved finding the nearest bridge. That tended to make people wonder if I was just a broke kid wandering across America.

"Well," she said, "let me ask Bobby if you can stay at our house." She called her boyfriend, who agreed without hesitation, so off we went.

When we arrived, Bobby showed me his massive red semi parked in his driveway. He showed me inside of the cabin, which was cool because I had never been in one before. Then Denise brought me into their home and showed me the guest room where I would be staying. I took a nice shower and changed into some clean clothes. After changing in my room, I got a call from a friend back home with heartbreaking news. Jasmine, the wife of Weyman Dodson—one of the men who helped baptize me—had passed away in a car accident the night before, on Monday, June 10, 2019.

I learned that the funeral would be in the next few days and decided to fly back to Greenville, South Carolina, to support my friend. Because my sister worked for United, it was possible. When I walked out of my room, I broke the news to Bobby and Denise. They were very understanding and supportive of my decision. That night, I called my sister, and she was able to get me on a flight out of Killeen the next day.

The next morning, I packed up my things and asked Denise if I could leave my longboard at their house. She said that was no problem. After a quick breakfast, Bobby drove me back to Lampasas, where Jenny picked me up and took me to Killeen. I spent the day with Jenny and Jeff before flying to South Carolina to attend Jasmine's funeral service on Sunday, June 16. It was heartbreaking to see her leave behind a husband and three young children. Her oldest, Grace, was only eight and had been in the passenger seat during the accident.

At the funeral, Grace bravely stood before the crowd and shared her last moments with her mother. Through tears, she said, "I just wanted everyone to know that I loved her so much, and I knew that she loved me because..." She stopped to wipe her eyes. "I don't remember anything from the accident, but someone told me she was found on top of me, saving my life." Her words pierced me. I had never seen a child endure so much and speak of it with such courage. It was a testimony of unconditional love that I will never forget.

After the funeral, I reconnected with friends I hadn't seen since the previous summer when I last lived in South Carolina. My friend Fratt lent me his Harley Davidson Softail, which was incredibly convenient since there were several friends I wanted to visit but had no vehicle.

The next day, Monday, June 17, I received the devastating news that another friend, Isai Francisco Cadalzo Sevilla, had died in Metairie, Louisiana. I met him while staying with Nate and Krista in New Orleans. I hadn't known him for long, but he was the type of guy who would remember you, showing that he genuinely cared. Unfortunately, I didn't receive any information about his funeral and couldn't attend.

The following day, I flew back to Texas to continue my journey west. Jenny kindly picked me up from the Killeen airport, and that evening, I stretched out on her couch and enjoyed a night of rest. I hadn't really thought through how I was going to get back to Brownwood, which was nearly two hours away by car, and I didn't want to ask Jenny to drive me. I mentioned in a social media post that I was headed that direction, and before long, a follower named Jerrod messaged me. He offered a private flight from the Austin airport to Brownwood if I could be there by Thursday afternoon. It was Tuesday night. Austin was farther in the opposite direction, but the thought of a private flight and meeting a new friend thrilled me. All I had to do was figure out how to get to Austin.

The next morning, I found out Jenny's daughter, Katie, and her boyfriend happened to be traveling to Austin for a party that night; it was perfect timing. They offered me a ride, so I jumped in their vehicle and headed to Austin with them. Unsure of where I would sleep Wednesday night, I posted a story on social media from the car as we drove to Austin. I asked if anyone in the area could host me for the night and take me to the airport the next day. By the time we arrived in Austin, Reid and Victoria had offered to host me again, so Katie dropped me off at their apartment. Then a stranger from Instagram named Madison volunteered to pick me up and take me to the airport on Thursday morning. Once again, I was amazed at how quickly God provided a solution to my predicament.

I was so thankful to Reid and Victoria for letting me stay another night in their home. The next day, Madison arrived at their apartment where we met for the first time. It was kinda hard for me to believe that this all came about from a social media post, but sure enough, she kindly drove me to the airport.

During the drive, I messaged Jerrod on Instagram, and he filled me in on the plan. He was flying into Austin from somewhere out east, returning home from college. Instead of making the drive, his parents decided to pick him up in their small plane. His stepdad, Chad, was a pilot and would be flying from Brownwood to Austin that morning and back later that day. Jerrod's mom, Dawn, tagged along to see her son for the first time in a while. After meeting up outside the main terminal, we headed over to the private side of the airport where the smaller aircraft take off.

Madison and I met Jerrod, Chad, and Dawn in the airport parking lot. There was an air of excitement as we all greeted each other. Madison and I said our goodbyes, and I gave her a big hug to thank her for the favor. After grabbing my backpack from Madison's car (my longboard was still at Bobby and Denise's house in Brownwood), she drove off, and I joined Jerrod, Chad, and Dawn inside the airport to access the runway. We followed Chad to his plane, a sleek white Beechcraft Bonanza with red pinstripes, wings, and tail, labeled N739MP. We loaded our bags, put on headsets, buckled in, and taxied out to the runway.

This wasn't my first time in a small aircraft, but it never gets old. The hum of the engine, the clear view through the windshield, and the tight quarters made it feel like an adventure right from the start. As we lifted off, Austin quickly faded beneath us, and we cruised westward across the Texas sky toward the small Brownwood airport. It was smooth flying and great company, exactly the kind of moment I never imagined being part of on this longboard trip, but one I'd never forget.

Upon landing, we were starving, so we went back to La Botana's for dinner. Chad had already invited me to stay the night at their house. Jerrod and I hit it off so well that they told me I was welcome to stay longer if I wanted. I decided to spend the weekend with him and his family. First, we stopped at Bobby and Denise's place to say hello and pick up my longboard. Then Jerrod and his friend gave me the grand tour of Brownwood, which included a trip to an old quarry that had filled with water and turned into a makeshift swimming hole with cliffs to jump from.

The water was deep, and the cliff was a solid fifteen feet. I jumped in with Jerrod's friend while Jerrod stayed on top; he wasn't in the mood to get wet. After climbing out, we sat on the ledge for a while, looking out over the water. It was scenic, peaceful, and the sort of place you forget exists until someone takes you there. From there, we headed to the disc golf course, where I proceeded to prove that my talent lay in longboarding, not in flinging plastic. Most of the round was spent thrashing through weeds and ivy trying to recover my disc.

That evening, Jerrod and I were outside shooting hoops as the sun dipped below the horizon. The warm twilight air made it easy to talk, and before long, our conversation drifted to some things he'd been carrying for a while—pain from his parents' divorce and the anger he couldn't seem to shake. I listened as he opened up, then gently asked if he wanted to hand it all over to Jesus and make Him the Lord of his life.

Jerrod paused for a moment, then said he did.

We set the basketball aside, and right there in the driveway, I placed my hand on his shoulder and prayed. I asked God to help him believe that the death and resurrection of Jesus could take away his pain and anger. Then I asked God to fill him with the Holy Spirit and told Jerrod to confess Jesus as the Lord of his life, and he did. It was a simple prayer, but the moment felt weighty. Jerrod stood quietly, and, through tears, he said he felt like a burden had been lifted off his shoulders.

Before heading in for the night, I encouraged him to get plugged into a local church and be baptized. It had been a powerful evening, one I hoped would mark a new beginning in his story.

The next morning, Monday, June 24, I woke up early to get ready to longboard. As I got out of bed, I noticed a rash on my arms and legs that looked suspiciously like poison ivy. It was so bad, I even filmed a short video of it. I remembered all the thrashing through weeds I had done while disc golfing and figured that must have been the culprit. Jerrod was getting ready for work and greeted me with a smile. "Good morning, Dan. Guess what happened last night after you went to bed?"

"What?" I asked, caught off guard.

"My mom was up when we came in, and she and I talked for over an hour about our past. It brought so much peace to our relationship."

"That's incredible!" I said.

"How did you sleep?" Jerrod asked.

"Well, I slept fine, but I woke up with this poison ivy rash," I replied, showing him my arms and legs.

When his mom came out to the kitchen, I showed her too. It was bad and seemed to be getting worse. They both felt sorry for me and offered to let me stay until it healed. Jerrod's mom handed me some Benadryl, and I took a shower, praying that God would heal me. By the time I stepped out, the house was empty, so I lay down on the couch and drifted off. When I woke up two hours later, the rash had completely vanished. I was stunned and had expected to be scratching for at least a week, but it was gone without a trace.

I uploaded before-and-after videos of my arms and legs to my social media, thinking people would be amazed at the sudden healing I'd experienced. While I was online, my heart sank. I saw a post from my friend's wife announcing that her husband, Trevor Heinrich, had just passed away from lung cancer that morning at 10:50 CST; he was only twenty-five years old.

Trevor was a friend I'd first met while living in Pennsylvania, the same one who had hoofed it across America with his friend, Jonathan Stoltzfus. When I met him, he was home for the holidays, somewhere in the middle of that trek, and preparing to fly back out to pick up where he'd left off. By the time he and Jon finished, I had spent time at both of their homes, happily listening to their stories and pretending to absorb their hard-earned wisdom while mostly marveling at the fact they were still able to walk. I was still wearing his neon safety vest most days as I skated my own way west.

Hearing that Trevor had passed on to be with Jesus brought a mixture of emotions. He had battled lung cancer for more than a year. When he found out he had stage 4 lung cancer in his early twenties, he was engaged to his fiancée, Stella. She still decided to marry him despite the diagnosis, which was a brave act of love. They were married for ten months before he passed away. Hearing of his death was heart-wrenching news. I knew I had to be there for his funeral in Pennsylvania. I called my sister again, and she was able to get me a flight out of Killeen.

When Jerrod got back from work, he shared how he had gone to his dad's house and had a deep, meaningful conversation. It brought him even more peace, lifting a weight off his heart and beginning the process of restoring their relationship.

"That's great news!" I told him. "God certainly has a way of working things out for good for those who love Him. Although sometimes we don't see it right away, like in the case of my friend, Trevor." Then I told Jerrod that he had just passed away that morning.

"I'm so sorry to hear that," Jerrod said.

"I'm going to fly back to Pennsylvania for the funeral. The flight leaves tomorrow morning from Killeen."

"Do you need a ride? I can drive you," Jerrod offered.

"That would be fantastic," I replied, and then I contacted Jenny to see if I could stay at her house before my flight. Of course, she was more than happy to host me again.

Soon I found myself in Pennsylvania for the second funeral and third death of a friend within the same month. Each had passed away exactly seven days apart, all in June, which felt like a mystery I could not unravel. Though I did not understand why, I trusted that God works all things together for good. Even the poison ivy rash that had delayed me at Jerrod's house turned out to be a blessing, because it gave me time to learn of Trevor's passing and make plans to attend his funeral before longboarding farther into West Texas. Somehow, God worked even that out for good.

Being at the funeral felt like exactly where I needed to be. I was able to support Trevor's family and wife, and I formed meaningful connections with people who have since become lifelong friends. The service was held in a large auditorium filled with nearly a thousand people. One person remarked that some people live an entire lifetime without making the kind of impact Trevor made in twenty-five years. I wholeheartedly agreed; Trevor lived like every moment was a precious gift from God, and he loved every person he encountered along the way, leaving a lasting impact on so many lives.

I used to imagine that life was long and full of endless opportunities, but now I believe each day is a gift meant to be lived with purpose and love. These funerals reminded me that life is short, and we never know when our time will come. It's best to live each day as if it is a gift. I look up to Trevor and want to leave a legacy as meaningful and far reaching as his, touching lives the way he did, with love and purpose. Imagine the impact we could all have if we lived by showing kindness to each person we encountered along life's journey.

CHAPTER 10.

THE LION, THE GARDEN & THE PROPHETIC DREAM

JULY 13 – SEPTEMBER 26, 2019
BROWNWOOD TO FARWELL, TEXAS

I used to imagine that miracles were rare and distant, but now I believe they can happen anywhere, often when we're keeping our eyes peeled and ears open to the heart of God.

After Trevor's funeral, I flew back to Texas. Jenny and Jeff dropped me off in Lampasas, and Bobby and Denise picked me up there and brought me back to Brownwood. Kelly, the hair salon lady, contacted me to let me know my new wheels had finally arrived. I visited her salon for another trim, and she gave me the new wheels. I removed my old ones, signed each with a silver Sharpie, and gifted them to a few friends who had supported my journey.

Bobby and Denise from the Early Visitor Center welcomed me back into their home. It was Saturday, July 13, and they were heading to an MLB game between the Texas Rangers and the Astros. They invited me along and even paid for my ticket. It turned out to be a nail-biter of a game, stretching to eleven innings before the Astros edged out a win by a single run.

The next morning, they brought me to their church. After the service, Jerrod picked me up to take me back to his place, where I had left my board before traveling to Trevor's funeral. When we arrived, his mom was in the kitchen. She gave me a hug, tears welling in her eyes. As she wiped them away, she told me my visit had made a real impact on her son and had strengthened their relationship. I hugged her back, silently thanking God for allowing me to play even a small part in their story.

The next morning, July 15, I was back on the road. I left Brownwood and headed to Coleman, Texas. Jenny had contacted the Coleman Chamber of Commerce and told me to stop by when I arrived. Becky Slayton from the Chamber of Commerce welcomed me to Coleman like I was family. She even handed me a Coleman T-shirt and said, with a smile, "Here, Dan, see if this fits you." I pulled it on, and it fit great.

We walked over to Owl Drug Store, a century-old local favorite with retro stools, checkered floors, and walls lined with vintage photos and soda fountain charm. The place was buzzing with conversation, and Becky seemed to know just about everyone.

"Oh hey, Pedro!" she called, waving him over. "You've gotta meet this guy; he's longboarding across the country!"

That's how it went. She introduced me to Bunkie, Pedro, and a girl named Alice who lived in Abilene, the next town west.

Alice smiled and told me, "If you end up coming through Abilene, I've got a couch you can sleep on. And my mom lives along the way; I'm sure she would be willing to host you too." I was blown away by the kindness. As we ate our food and sipped sweet tea, I kept thinking how places like this made the miles worth it. It wasn't just lunch; it was a moment of real hospitality I'd never forget.

After we finished eating, Becky introduced me to various people around town. We met the fire chief at the fire station, visited the local newspaper, and even shook hands with the mayor. Afterward, Becky dropped me off at the Coleman Inn, where a local pastor had generously offered to cover my stay. I felt deeply honored he would do that for me.

The hotel had an outdoor pool, so I took full advantage and went for a dip; it was glorious. Becky had mentioned that the pastor of a cowboy church wanted to meet me, and before long, I got a call from him. His name was Seth and he invited me to join him that night for Celebrate Recovery at his church, which, fittingly, was an old gas station they had converted into a sanctuary.

At one point, we broke into small groups. My group headed into another room, and on the chair I chose was a small card with a rainbow lion painted on it. Across the bottom, in bold white letters, were the words I LOVE YOU. I've always loved lions, so it felt as if God Himself had tucked that card there for me.

After the service concluded, Seth brought me back to the inn. It was nice to have a room all to myself. I counted up all the money that people had donated to me that day for my trip; it was $135. After journaling and getting ready for bed, I slipped under the covers and fell asleep.

Early the next morning, around 5 a.m., I left Coleman and headed north toward Abilene. About fifteen miles up the road, I stopped in the tiny town of Novice and met up with Alice for breakfast at a local café. Over coffee and eggs, she told me her parents lived on a big piece of land along my route and would be willing to host me for the night. I accepted the invite, and Alice gave me her mom's contact info.

After breakfast, Alice headed to work in Abilene, and I longboarded the rest of the way to her parents' property. Her mom, Emma, greeted me warmly at the door, showed me where I could take a shower, and let me crash on the couch to rest. The property was expansive, with wide pastures, a corral, and several horses that Alice grew up riding. Though she lived in Abilene now, she came back often to ride and spend time with the animals she loved.

That afternoon, once Alice got off work, she returned and saddled up two of the horses for us. We rode through the pastures for well over an hour. The sun was low in the sky, casting golden light over the field of grass as we trotted along. It was the longest I had ever ridden a horse, and I loved every second of it.

When we returned to the house, Emma had dinner waiting for us. I don't remember exactly what she cooked, maybe steak or grilled chicken, but it was hearty and delicious. Afterward, we stayed up for a little while chatting before I thanked them and headed to bed because I was planning to get up early the next morning. As I got up from the table to walk toward the guest room, I said my goodbyes so that I could be ready to slip out in the morning. "Be safe out there," Emma said with a kind smile. "And don't forget to come and visit again."

"Thanks for your hospitality and the delicious dinner. Y'all are great hosts."

Alice said, "Don't let that Texas sun roast you too bad. I'll see you tomorrow, Daniel. Sleep well."

Alice and I had arranged for me to longboard to her house in Abilene the next morning. She had a couch for me to sleep on and was only about 35 miles (56 kilometers) northwest of her parents' house. She left that night to go home, and I went straight to sleep.

The next morning, I stood up at 3:30, quietly packed my things, and got ready to head out. With a grateful heart and a rested body, I set out toward Abilene. I started riding at 4 a.m. to beat the heat and followed Highway 84 north toward Abilene. While I rode, I listened to a mix of podcasts by Pastor Bill Johnson, Levi Lusko, and the Bible Project. One of the messages was about faith, and it stirred something deep inside me. It bolstered my spirit as I pushed forward, assuring me that I was living the life I was meant to live. By the time I finished listening, the sun was rising in the east, casting pink, red, and orange hues across the sky. It was like a visual echo of the encouragement I felt inside. Maybe it was the sermons or maybe it was the majestic sky, but I felt compelled to ask God for something I hadn't ever asked for—I asked to see a miracle.

The air was cool, and the roads were smooth, allowing me to move at a good clip, around ten miles per hour. After 35 miles, I arrived at Alice's house in Abilene at 7 a.m. and knocked on her front door.

"Oh, hi, Daniel," Alice said. "Good morning. What time did you leave?"

"Hey, Alice, good morning. I left around four. I made good time because of the smooth roads."

"I'm making some breakfast now. Come in and eat. I have to go to work soon. But you can make yourself at home."

With that, Alice gave me a quick tour of the house and pointed out the couch I could sleep on. Not long after, she headed off to work. Soon a local ABC news reporter showed up at her place to interview me, and while the camera was rolling, Emma arrived. When we wrapped up the interview, I tagged along with her as she ran a few errands around town. Later that afternoon, Emma dropped me back at Alice's just as Alice was pulling in from work. "Hey, do you want to go to a worship night in the park that a local church is hosting?" she asked. "It's just down the street."

"That sounds great."

As I waited for Alice to get ready, I wrote in my journal: "God, please provide for my needs. Help me to be at the right place at the right time to meet the right person." I was almost out of money, but as always, I prayed and trusted God to move.

When Alice was ready, we walked over to the park and met up with some of her friends. The event had just started, and people were on the stage singing. After a couple of songs, a lady introduced the band, made some announcements, and then said, "I have some bad news. Our speaker can't make it. And our backup speaker just called and told us they can't make it either, so we are asking God for a miraculous word tonight. If anyone feels like they should share something, come talk with me during the next song."

Immediately, I felt compelled to share about my longboard trip and how God had always provided for me. I spoke with the lady, and she approved of my message. After a few other people spoke, I found myself standing on a stage in front of about fifty people. I'm not uncomfortable speaking in public, but I also wasn't used to it. I was a little nervous at first, but I knew God wanted me to do it. "Hi, everyone," I began. "I'm Daniel, and I'm longboarding across America, sharing the love of God as I go." I told them how I had stepped out in faith and didn't even carry a tent. I shared how God had been faithfully providing me places to stay and money for food during my journey. After I finished and was walking off the platform, I exchanged smiles with a lady with short, bright orange hair who was walking up to speak next.

She shared about how she was in a church service once where a blank canvas and paints and brushes were set up in front of the stage. People were encouraged to come up and create something. She told us how she hadn't painted in a long time. Nevertheless, she courageously went forward, picked up the brush, and painted a rainbow lion. Then she told us how she had put that painting onto small cards and wrote the words I LOVE YOU in bold white letters.

I was shocked. I had seen her card at the cowboy church just a few days before and wondered who had painted that lion, and now the artist was standing before me, telling the story of how she painted it. Later, when things were winding down, I went over to introduce myself. "Hi, I'm Daniel, what was your name?"

"I'm Latimer. It's nice to meet you," she said.

"I can't believe I'm meeting you. The other day I was in a church in Coleman and saw one of your cards."

"No way! That is so cool! I'm so glad to meet you." She proceeded to ask me questions about my longboard trip. While we were talking, Alice came over. Earlier that day, she had mentioned that she had been praying for her brother to come to Jesus. I asked Latimer if she would pray with Alice. Soon her friends came to join us, and we all held hands and prayed for different things. Latimer spoke words of encouragement to us, and after that, it was time to leave. Before we walked away, Latimer pulled me aside and said, "I feel like God wants me to do something for you." She proceeded to hand me $120, an answer to my earlier prayer request. God is good.

As we walked away, one of Alice's friends mentioned that her mom and stepdad lived on a big ranch farther west, near Sweetwater. They had a garden and grew organic produce. She mentioned that they might be willing to host me as I continued west. She offered to connect us, and soon the arrangements were set. I would spend the weekend in Abilene and then longboard out to their ranch early the next week. Since their place was off the beaten path, we agreed someone would pick me up from the main road.

On Tuesday, July 23, I left Alice's place at 5 a.m. and began riding west on I-20 toward Sweetwater. About an hour and a half in, Jason—one of the guys who helped out at the garden—texted to say he was headed to the ranch and could swing by to pick me up. I had met him at Alice's house church gathering on Sunday and saved his number. True to his word, Jason pulled over on the shoulder, rolled down the window with a big grin, and told me to toss my board in the back. He chatted easily as we drove, asking about my trip and pointing out landmarks along the way, the kind of person who makes you feel like you've known him longer than a couple of days. I was especially thankful, because the ranch was many miles off my route, and their gravel driveway stretched on for what felt like forever. When we finally pulled up and stepped out of the car, Elizabeth greeted us warmly and introduced me to her husband, Keith, and their dog, Copper.

After getting a short tour of the place, we began working in the garden. We harvested peaches, blackberries, raspberries, beets, tomatoes, onions, garlic, and more, and then enjoyed some of them for lunch. Elizabeth was a great cook, and almost everything we ate came straight from their garden. That afternoon, once all the work was done, we made salsa and ate it with some tortilla chips, which is one of my favorite combinations. Keith and Elizabeth's salsa recipe was exceptional, making a good afternoon snack.

Once Jason headed back to Abilene, Keith and Elizabeth showed me the guest room where I would sleep. The room was quaint, with a bed, lamp, and dresser. Just outside the door was a table and chair that would be perfect for writing in my journal. It was all so comfortable, and I was incredibly thankful.

As evening came, Elizabeth started making dinner from some of the garden produce we harvested that day. After we ate, Keith and Elizabeth wanted to show me around the ranch. We all fit on their UTV (utility terrain vehicle) and began driving around. Keith was going a decent speed on one of the few gravel roads that was beyond their house, when suddenly, he abruptly stopped the vehicle and said, "There's an arrowhead!" At first, his words didn't register with me until I realized that this used to be an area occupied by Native Americans. I couldn't believe that he had spotted an arrowhead in the road while driving so fast, but sure enough, he jumped out of the UTV and picked up a perfect white arrowhead. After examining it, Keith handed it to me. Keith continued driving until we reached a spot overlooking a large valley. The sun was getting ready to set, and the scenery was beautiful. Soon we got back in the UTV and returned to their house.

Back at the house, as we sat on their comfy furniture in the living room, Keith asked me, "Daniel, can you interpret dreams?"

"Did you have a dream recently?" I asked.

He told me, "Yeah, I actually had a dream this morning just before you came."

In the Bible, Daniel was a dream interpreter, so I wondered if I could be too. Then I asked Keith to tell me his dream. He leaned back in his recliner and began to recall the dream. "I was at a Bible study with Elizabeth when the leader of the group asked me to read 2 Kings chapter 4 verse 8. I didn't have my own Bible with me, so I used Elizabeth's and began searching for the Scripture. But I couldn't find it because there were no headings in her Bible. I kept trying, and then I woke up."

"Well," I said, "what does 2 Kings 4:8 say?"

"Why don't you get your Bible and read it?" Keith told me.

As I went to my room to grab my Bible, Keith mentioned that he had read the verse right when he woke up. I came back into the living room, sat on the couch, and opened my Bible to 2 Kings 4:8. "If you notice," Keith said, "the first verse is the beginning of a story, so why don't you just read the whole thing?"

As I looked at the passage, I noticed that I had underlined some verses from the last time I read this passage in Florida. It was around the same time I had underlined the story of Elijah receiving bread from ravens, which coincided with a raven dropping bread for me. Here is what the passage says, with the underlined verses matching those in my personal Bible (ESV):

> 8 One day Elisha went on to Shunem, where a wealthy
> woman lived, who urged him to eat some food. So
> whenever he passed that way, he would turn in there to eat
> food. 9 And she said to her husband, "Behold now, I know
> that this is a holy man of God who is continually passing
> our way. 10 Let us make a small room on the roof with walls
> and put there for him a bed, a table, a chair, and a lamp, so
> that whenever he comes to us, he can go in there."

At this point I began smiling while reading because of the stark similarities of this Bible story and my own current circumstances.

> [11] One day he came there, and he turned into the chamber and rested there. [12] And he said to Gehazi, his servant, "Call this Shunammite." When he had called her, she stood before him.[13] And he said to him, "Say now to her, 'See, you have taken all this trouble for us; what is to be done for you? Would you have a word spoken on your behalf to the king or to the commander of the army?'" She answered, "I dwell among my own people."[14] And he said, "What then is to be done for her?" Gehazi answered, "Well, she has no son, and her husband is old."[15] He said, "Call her." And when he had called her, she stood in the doorway.[16] And he said, "At this season, about this time next year, you shall embrace a son." And she said, "No, my lord, O man of God; do not lie to your servant."[17] But the woman conceived, and she bore a son about that time the following spring, as Elisha had said to her.

That was the end of the paragraph, so I stopped reading and looked up at Keith and Elizabeth, who were both staring at me intently. "What do you think it means, Daniel?" Keith asked.

My mind paired the similarities of the story and to me arriving at Keith and Elizabeth's house and them offering me a room as I traveled through just like the prophet in the story. Although Elizabeth had a daughter from her prior marriage, Keith and Elizabeth had no children of their own. Our circumstances were so similar to that of the story's that I jokingly responded, "Well, I guess Elizabeth is going to have a baby!" It was a lighthearted response considering that Elizabeth seemed to be past her child-bearing years.

"God's promised me a son, Daniel," Elizabeth replied, her tone suddenly serious.

"Oh," I responded, shifting to match her demeanor. "How has He done that?"

"Well, through a number of ways. First off, Keith and I have never been able to have a child together. We've been praying for a son for a long time, and different people have prophesied over me that I would have a son. Hebrews 11:11 has always encouraged me when I would read the verse. It says, 'And by faith even Sarah, who was past childbearing age, was enabled to bear children because she considered Him faithful who had made the promise,' This verse had been stuck in my mind for a while when my daughter painted me a picture of three unhatched eggs in a bird's nest. To me, it represented the three miscarriages I've had with Keith. What really struck me was that my daughter painted it on November 11 and wrote 11/11 in the bottom corner of the painting. I felt like it was a confirmation of the prophecies I had received."

"Then, about a year ago," she continued, "I looked up in the sky and saw a cloud that looked just like a baby in the womb. The sun was directly behind it. The cloud was white, and the part that looked like the baby was blue. It was like God was telling me Himself that I was to have a baby boy. It was so unique that I took a picture of it."

"Could I see this picture?" I asked. Elizabeth went to look for it and pulled it up on their laptop. The image was unmistakably in the shape of a baby in the womb, its tiny form outlined within a faint white cloud behind it. As we studied the image closer, we noticed that the cloud bore a striking resemblance to the arrowhead Keith had found just hours earlier. When I pointed it out, we were all shocked.

Then Keith searched for something on his phone and read, "Like arrows in the hand of a warrior, so are the children of one's youth. Happy is the man who has his quiver full of them (Psalms 127:4-5)." It was like God Himself was tying the arrowhead and the image of the child together right before our eyes.

Elizabeth said to me, "Whenever people would prophecy about the baby, I used to joke that I'd have it when I turned fifty, well, I'm fifty this year, Daniel."

It seemed like there were so many signs pointing to the idea that Elizabeth would have a son, with the central one being Keith's dream that morning. To top it all off, Keith and Elizabeth told me that they had already chosen a name for the son they believed they would have. They had decided on this name a while ago, wanting to honor Keith's great-grandfather; his name was Daniel.

We ended the evening in prayer, asking for God's will to be done and for Elizabeth's baby to come. The signs seemed too clear to ignore. That night, I sat at the table and recorded every detail in my journal. As I lay down on my bed, I couldn't help but be in awe of it all. Staring at the ceiling, I thought about how miraculous it would be if Elizabeth did have a son. The entire night felt supernatural, and I was deeply thankful for the experience, eagerly anticipating what might happen.

The next morning, we had breakfast before heading out to the garden to harvest some vegetables. In the afternoon, Keith and Elizabeth took me on a tour of a different part of the ranch. They wanted to introduce me to the owner, so we stopped at his house and knocked on his door. His name was Randy, and he had a beautiful home. As he showed me around, I noticed a large painting above the fireplace mantel. It was the same rainbow lion I had seen a week ago! Curious, I asked him about it, and he told me that the artist, Latimer, had painted it for him, and he loved it so much that he proudly displayed it there. I mentioned to him that I had the opportunity to meet her, and he was surprised. He asked me about my trip, and I shared some stories of the adventures I had been on so far. Randy was so impressed by the journey I was on that he generously gave me $100, which was a significant boost to my finances.

I ended up staying on the ranch for a week, enjoying a wonderful time of rest and rejuvenation. When it was time for me to leave, Keith and Elizabeth drove me back to the same highway that Jason had originally picked me up. We took a photo together and then said our goodbyes.

I continued my journey west through Snyder, Lubbock, and all the way to Muleshoe, nearing the New Mexico border where the town of Farwell, Texas waited for me. Jenny kept calling ahead to each town, letting them know I was coming, which led to many more interviews. Because of all the attention, I never had to sleep outside. Everywhere I went, someone offered to host me. It felt like yet another miracle, and I'm incredibly grateful for all the amazing people I met and those who opened their homes to me throughout West Texas.

Later in my journey, on October 21, I decided to give Keith and Elizabeth a call to check in and say hello. When Elizabeth picked up, she had some surprising news to share with me. "After you left the ranch," she said, "we went on vacation to Colorado. While we were there, I conceived, and now I'm pregnant."

"What! That's incredible," I exclaimed, a bit shocked, but super excited. "God really did give us so many signs, though, so I guess we shouldn't be surprised."

Keith and Elizabeth were overjoyed. After everything they had been through, this news was a blessing. I congratulated them, and we spent some more time chatting and catching up. I shared where I was on my journey, and we updated each other on our lives. Before we ended the call, we prayed together and then said goodbye.

A few months went by, and I hadn't heard much from Keith and Elizabeth, so I called them up again to check in, only to be met with heartbreaking news. Elizabeth told me that on October 31, she miscarried. I was stunned and didn't know how to respond. Elizabeth spoke up and shared something she had been encouraged by. She said, "At the end of the book of Job, he gets back double everything he lost, except for his children. Job lost seven thousand sheep and three thousand camels, and God gave him fourteen thousand sheep and six thousand camels. But Job lost seven children, and instead of receiving fourteen more, he only got seven. That's because his children live on in eternity, and Job would be reunited with them one day. Just like Job, I will be reunited with my baby someday. God promised me a child, and He gave me one; I just haven't met him yet."

Elizabeth's faith and perspective in the face of such loss remained steadfast. She truly believed that God was working all things together for good. As I continued my journey, the words she spoke stayed with me, reminding me that God's promises often unfold in ways we least expect. The story of Keith and Elizabeth wasn't just about hope for a son they could one day hold in their arms; it was about unshakable trust in God's plan, even when it veers into the unknown. Their faith in God gave me strength as I pressed on, knowing that every push I took on my longboard was part of a greater story being written: a story I often experienced only in fragments.

You see, back in Florida when I prayed for Bible stories to happen in my life, I never imagined they would look like this. Yet here I was in Texas, living out a story that mirrored the very scriptures I had underlined in Florida. God was answering my prayers yet again.

After I got off the phone with Elizabeth, I thought about all the signs and circumstances of what we experienced and discovered back at the ranch. I was sad to hear that her baby had died before it had even lived. Then I went back to read 2 Kings chapter 4 again. I rediscovered that the story didn't end with the birth of a promised son. It continues and says that when the boy was grown, his life was taken from him, and he died in his mother's lap. Then Elisha returns to the Shunammite woman's home and raises her son back to life. It's a story of restoration, faith, and a radical miracle that defies all human understanding. It's a story that also points to Jesus. I used to imagine that miracles were rare and distant, but now I believe they can happen anywhere, often when we're keeping our eyes peeled and ears open to the heart of God.

I often wonder if I still have a role to play in Elizabeth's story, if perhaps, like Elisha, I'm meant to intercede in a way that helps fulfill God's plan. The thought has stayed with me through the years, and I've been praying about it ever since. It's always struck me that in the Bible, Daniel was a dream interpreter, and Elizabeth conceived a child in her old age. If God did a miracle then, He can surely do it again.

This experience deepened my faith and reminded me of the power of prayer, prophecy, and God's ability to work miracles. I hold onto the hope that Elizabeth's story isn't finished yet and that, in some small way, I could be a part of the unfolding of God's promises in Keith and Elizabeth's life. Isaiah 64:4 reminds us that no eye has seen, nor ear has heard of a God like Yahweh. He is the One who acts for those who wait for Him.

CHAPTER 11.

THE FIRST BIG FALL WITH BLOOD ON MY HANDS

SEPTEMBER 27 — OCTOBER 21, 2019

FARWELL, TEXAS TO GALLUP, NEW MEXICO

I used to imagine that challenges slowed the journey,
but now I believe that they enrich the experience.

On Friday, September 27, 2019, I crossed the Texas–New Mexican border on my longboard, passing through the town of Farwell, Texas. It was a huge milestone for me. The distance from Deweyville—where I first entered the state—to Farwell is an eleven-hour drive by car. It took me nearly four months to get there. Crossing that state line was a moment of triumph, a testament to how far I'd come. I took a picture next to the welcome sign that said, THE LAND OF ENCHANTMENT. My route had taken me from Muleshoe to Farwell, Texas, and then into Texico, New Mexico. But now, I was eager to finish the trip and aimed to reach my destination by the end of the year, or even by Thanksgiving if possible.

New Mexico had a distinctly different vibe that I couldn't quite explain, but I could feel it. Perhaps it was because the state was entirely new to me. I had never been there before and didn't know anyone. Fortunately, my friend Jonathan Stoltzfus, who had walked across America with Trevor Heinrich, offered to connect me with some friends in Moriarty, a town east of Albuquerque. This gave me a sense of comfort as I prepared to navigate through this unfamiliar terrain.

My first day in New Mexico was an adventure in the truest sense of the word. I had almost no money, didn't know a soul, and was traveling without a tent. The wind was so strong that if I stood still on my longboard, it carried me backward like some cheap amusement park ride. Determined to move forward, I pushed westward late into the afternoon. As the sun began to sink, the wind finally died down, and I found myself somewhere between Clovis and Fort Sumner. To my left, a freight train stretched endlessly across the horizon as the sky turned every shade of fire and ash—reds, oranges, streaks of violet and blue. Golden grass rippled along the roadside, the land so flat it felt like I could see the curvature of the earth. It was one of the most spectacular sunsets I'd ever seen, and I was too tired to fully appreciate it.

By then, I had logged more than fifty miles, with thirty still to go before reaching Fort Sumner. The landscape offered nothing but dusty emptiness, the occasional scrubby bush, and a growing sense that I had made a terrible decision to continue with this trip. Fatigue set in, and I actually considered curling up behind one of those bushes to sleep. Just then a massive tarantula lumbered across the road. I don't know if you've ever seen a tarantula in the wild, but they move with the sort of casual authority that suggests they already own the place. I panicked, of course, because spiders and I have never been on good terms. The idea of lying down anywhere near one was immediately off the table. Suddenly, I had a fresh surge of motivation to keep moving.

By the time I rolled into Fort Sumner, I had covered eighty-three miles. My legs felt like wood, my feet were on fire, and I was so exhausted I could have cried if I'd had the energy. I hunted for food, but at midnight, the whole town was shut down tight. Dinner was reduced to two granola bars and an apple from my pack. With my stomach grumbling, I turned to the next challenge: finding a place to sleep that did not involve tarantulas. Eventually, I stumbled upon a bench tucked behind a row of commercial buildings in the center of town. Not exactly the Ritz, but it worked. I collapsed there and slept from midnight until 5 a.m., grateful for a horizontal surface and the relative absence of eight-legged company.

When I woke up, I dug out a few snacks from my backpack and headed to a gas station to restock on food and water. My next stop was Santa Rosa, where I planned to catch Interstate 40 toward Moriarty. Getting there took the entire morning; it was 46 long miles without so much as a gas station to refill water. By the end, one of my shoes had split open at the sole, proof that I had now logged 130 miles in just 32 hours.

Hungry and determined to find food, I made a beeline for the first restaurant in sight, a Subway tucked inside a truck stop off Highway 84 at the edge of Santa Rosa. A sandwich never tasted so good. Afterward, I saw on Google Maps that the town had a freshwater spring called the Blue Hole, so I limped over and dove in. The cool water was like medicine, reviving me enough to think about where to sleep. Without my bivy, my only option was the inflatable mattress I carried, so I hauled it under the I-40 bridge, cracked open a can of Chef Boyardee ravioli, and chased it down with a bag of Dollar General tortilla chips. This was my gourmet combo across America. Then I stretched out under the overpass, full, exhausted, and oddly content.

The next day, Sunday, I slept longer than expected, but it was needed because I was wiped out. I finally rolled off my little air mattress around 10 a.m. and spent the rest of the day taking it easy, trying to figure out my next move. Moriarty was 80 miles (129 kilometers) away on I-40, with nothing but wasteland in between. To make matters worse, the weather app showed a storm heading straight for Santa Rosa the next day. As much as I wanted to stay another night, I knew I had to keep moving if I wanted to avoid the weather.

I also knew that trying to tackle eighty miles in the daytime under the New Mexican sun would roast me alive and leave me drained long before I got there. So around 6:45 p.m., without overthinking it, I packed up my gear, jumped on my longboard, and rolled onto the I-40 on-ramp, hoping the night air would give me just enough edge to make it.

If road conditions were good, I could manage about 8 miles per hour, which meant I was looking at least a 10-hour ride, if not 15. This would be my second attempt at longboarding through the entire night. I wasn't sure what to expect, but I knew God was with me.

As the sun slipped below the horizon like it always did, the temperature dropped, and I rolled deeper into the barren emptiness of New Mexico. Google Maps promised a twenty-four-hour gas station about halfway along my route, and I pinned all my hopes on it for food and water. The desert around me was nearly pitch black, broken only by the glare of oncoming headlights and the red streaks of taillights disappearing into the distance. Overhead, the stars flared bright in the clear sky, a reminder that separation from civilization can sometimes be beautiful.

I stuck to the right shoulder, and every time a semi roared past, the gust of wind shoved me forward like an impatient older brother. My headlamp lit maybe ten feet ahead, which wasn't much comfort, and although I wore Trevor's neon vest, my black backpack blocked most of its visibility from behind. As I pushed on into the dark, I prayed I wouldn't be clipped by a truck; that would be quite the headline for the newspapers reporting my journey.

The entire route was a subtle uphill climb, the elevation rising as the humidity plummeted. The air grew so dry, it hurt to breathe through my nose. I'd recently found a red, blue, and yellow silk bandana on a gravel road and tied it around my face just to make breathing bearable. By the time I reached the gas station, it was midnight. The place was dark, doors locked, lights out. I stood there staring, completely disheartened. "I thought this was open twenty-four hours?" I muttered. Google Maps, it turned out, meant the pumps, not the store, and I had just discovered this the hard way. Exhausted, I considered stopping, but with the temperature hovering at forty-eight degrees (8.9°C), sleeping outside wasn't an option. Hypothermia was a possibility, and besides, I was too cold to even imagine drifting off to sleep.

To stay warm, I pulled an extra T-shirt from my backpack and layered it over the one I was already wearing. I had a long-sleeve shirt and pants with me, but I left them buried in the bag. At the time, I figured it would waste precious minutes to dig them out, and if I just kept moving, the longboarding would generate enough heat to keep me alive. Looking back, I realize I should have just taken the time. My face took the brunt of the cold, especially with the headwind. My lips and cheeks dried out so fast that, in desperation, I wrapped an extra pair of underwear around my face like some makeshift balaclava. Then, with no other choice, I pushed west into the cold, dark night.

At 1:45 a.m., a green mileage sign informed me that Moriarty was still 34 miles (55 kilometers) away. I was exhausted but had no choice except to keep going. The next four hours were the hardest of the entire trip. The highway stretched on endlessly, mile after mile in the biting air. By 4 a.m., a billboard appeared out of the darkness: CLINES CORNERS—OPEN 24/7—EXIT NOW. Far in the distance, the lights of a truck stop glowed like a city on a hill, promising warmth and coffee. I forced myself forward until I finally rolled up to the doors. When I stepped off the board, my legs trembled under me; after so many hours of pushing, walking felt unnatural.

The first thing I did was made a beeline to the bathroom to run warm water over my hands like it was a miracle cure. Then I walked over to the hand dryer to warm up my body and let the hot air battle the chill out of my fingers. *I didn't give up,* I thought to myself and felt a sense of accomplishment as I waited for the dryer to stop. Then I bought a massive burrito, which I demolished in record time. Sitting on a bench in the truck stop, I could barely keep my eyes open from sheer exhaustion. With twenty-three more miles to Moriarty, I seriously considered calling Jonathan's friend to come rescue me, but I knew that I would regret abandoning my longboard. I was on a mission, so I pushed on.

Around 5 a.m., I got back on my board and watched the sunrise come up behind me. From Clines Corners to Moriarty, the road was mostly downhill, and the temperature was slowly rising. This was enough to give me a new burst of energy, and I somehow managed to complete the last twenty-three miles with surprising ease. On the horizon, for the first time since Florida, real mountains rose up; the Sandia range emerged in the distance like a promise and a warning all at once. Up until then, my route had been flatter than a pancake, so the idea of climbing felt both daunting and oddly thrilling.

This night stretch of the trip was one of the toughest for me personally. I had climbed 3,000 feet (914 meters) in elevation and longboarded over 80 miles in 15 consecutive hours, all in 48-degree weather while wearing a shoe whose sole was trying to make a burst for freedom.

Jonathan had given me the number of his friend Mike, a pastor at a Calvary Chapel Church just south of Moriarty. We arranged to meet at a park in the center of town, and by the time I arrived, it was close to 10 a.m. on Monday morning. I had been awake for nearly twenty-four hours. Mike pulled up in a black F-150. "Hey, I'm Mike. You must be Daniel," he said as he got out of the truck. I slowly stood up from the park bench I had been waiting on and probably looked a mess.

"Yeah, I'm Daniel. Hi. It's nice to meet you."

"So you just longboarded through the entire night, huh?"

"Yes, about eighty miles, and it got really cold and dry."

"Well, we've got you covered, my friend. Back at the church, you can take a hot shower, and we've got a place for you to sleep as well. Here, let me give you a hand." Mike grabbed my backpack and board and put them in the back seat of his truck. As we drove to his place, he asked me about my trip and told me about his church. It wasn't a big church, and his wife and two daughters lived in a fifth wheel on the property. When we got to his place, he introduced me to his wife, Liana, and their daughters, Rhema and Torah.

Since they didn't have a guest room, they put me in the church nursery. Liana had turned an air mattress into something resembling a king's bed, tucking it in with soft sheets and a warm blanket. After a quick shower, I collapsed onto it and was asleep before my head hit the pillow. The room was pitch black, the blankets perfectly warm, and the temperature just cool enough to be ideal, so I slept most of the day. That evening, I joined Mike and his family at a church member's house for a small group, where we rounded things out with fried pastries called sopapillas. Even after such a long nap, I slept without trouble that night.

The following day was Tuesday, October 1. I was reading my Bible when two homeless guys, Greg and Eric, came to the church to take showers. Liana had washed my clothes the night before and folded them in a nice stack on the chair. When Greg walked by, he asked me, "Are these clothes free?"

"These are *my* clothes," I told him, emphasizing the smaller truth that I didn't plan to give them away.

After he left, a subtle nudge from God told me to offer my clothes to him and Eric. I grabbed my stack of clothes and walked outside. "Hey, man," I called to him. "If you guys need some clothes, you can take what you need." They took everything, even my balaclava underwear, and stuffed them in their bags without so much as to try them on. Then Mike pulled up in his truck to give Greg and Eric a ride into town, unaware that I had just emptied my suitcase. They climbed in the back seat, and I hopped in the front. When we dropped them off, God led me to also give each of them $20, so I did, but it wasn't easy. I don't remember whether either of them said thank you, but I was reminded of Jesus's teaching to give to those who cannot repay you, even when the only reward is knowing you obeyed (Luke 14:12–14).

It may have seemed crazy to give away every piece of clothing I owned, but I did it in faith, trusting God to provide. By the end of the day, He did just that. Unaware I had emptied my bag, several people who had been following my journey sent a total of $350 through a money transfer app. One specifically gave me money for new shoes. It felt like a quiet confirmation that when we seek God's kingdom first, our needs are met, often in ways we cannot predict. I said goodbye to Greg and Eric, a little lighter in luggage, but a lot fuller in faith.

That night, Mike and Liana took me to a Peruvian restaurant in Albuquerque with their daughters, and we enjoyed a delicious meal together. Rhema would not stop making funny faces at me and carrying on before the food came out. When it did, Mike said, with wide eyes, "I'm so excited for this, you don't even know." I ordered a dish with tender sauteed chicken, red onions, and a side of vibrant green cilantro rice stacked high in a pyramid shape for reasons only known to the chef. It came with creamy orange huancaína-style sauce and was packed with flavor. The table was full of food, laughter, good conversation, and tall glasses of ice water.

When we finished eating, Mike picked up the bill, and I made sure to thank him properly. Back at the church, I settled into the nursery for a long, grateful sleep. I had loved my time with them and felt spoiled by their hospitality, but by morning, I was ready to press on. Mike, Liana, and the girls urged me to stay longer, and Rhema even cried when I left, which made saying goodbye more difficult than I liked.

I longboarded 18 miles through a pass in the Sandia Mountains, following the old path of Route 66. The incline was steady but manageable, winding between weathered rock formations and scattered patches of brush. The traffic was light, and the cool mountain air brushed against my face as

I pushed forward. It wasn't a dramatic climb, but it was just enough to give my legs a good workout.

Some friends I stayed with in Muleshoe, Texas, connected me to my next hosts, Fran and Brian. Their home was conveniently located just off the road I was traveling and nestled into the side of a mountain. That night, Fran cooked up a delicious and hearty beef stew that satisfied the hunger I developed from my journey that day. The following morning, I took a walk around their property, which was a peaceful and nice place to rest. I didn't stay long before hopping back on my board and heading to my next host's house, which was on the west side of Albuquerque.

During my longboarding journey across America, I practiced pushing with both legs to develop my muscles evenly. Typically, I rode with my left foot forward, known as the "regular" stance, but when your right foot is forward, it's called riding "goofy." Despite the name, there's nothing wrong with it. Some of the world's greatest skaters, including Tony Hawk, ride goofy. But if I ride goofy, it's like writing with your non-dominant hand. It feels unnatural and takes time to master. That's what I was working on throughout my trip, switching between stances to improve my "ambipedalness."

That morning, everything felt like it was finally falling into place. I had just stayed with some nice people, I was making great progress west, and the weather was perfect—sunny, crisp, and cool enough to keep me from overheating. Cruising along the legendary Route 66, I soaked in the moment. The Sandia Mountains towered around me like a painted backdrop, and I paused often to snap photos and record short videos, capturing the beauty and the quiet freedom of the open road.

It felt like one of those rare days when the world obligingly behaves, everything just clicks, and you briefly allow yourself to believe that you might be clever enough to do this forever.

As the road curved through the pass, I started descending a long, steady hill. For practice, I switched my stance and rode goofy, something I'd done before but never on a slope this steep. At first, it felt smooth and effortless. The wind rushed past my ears, and I let myself relax into the speed. Then I noticed a stoplight ahead, coming up faster than I expected. I was probably going about fifteen miles an hour and realized too late that I hadn't planned for how I'd slow down.

I panicked. I tried dragging my left foot to brake, but it threw off my balance. In a blink, I flew off the board and smashed the asphalt with my bare hands. My palms scraping hard against the pavement before my body rolled under the heavy thud of my backpack. When I came to a stop, the sting hit me, and blood was already dripping from both my hands. I scrambled to get up as fast as I could, but my palms were a mess, badly scraped, bleeding, and embedded with bits of gravel. A few items spilled from my backpack and sprawled across the road as cars swerved to miss them. I scooped them up as fast as a kid beneath a busted piñata, desperate to rescue them before passing tires turned them into road debris.

Somehow, the palms of my hands were the only thing injured, but they looked rough. I glanced around, realizing I didn't even know where my longboard had ended up. I took a quick video to explain what had just happened and thanked God that I wasn't injured more severely. Then I walked across the intersection and found my board beyond the parking lot of a store. I asked the clerk inside if I could use the bathroom to wash my hands.

After that, I longboarded to a drug store to buy hydrogen peroxide, Neosporin, gauze, and some adhesive tape to wrap up my hands. The pain was settling in, and I knew I needed to take care of the scrapes before I continued my trip. I called Pastor Mike to let him know what had happened. Without hesitation, he offered to pick me up and host me at the church until my hands healed. It wasn't long before he pulled up in his black F-150 again—this time, Rhema was in the back seat. Her little face lit up when she saw me, thrilled to see me again.

Once we got back to the church, Liana helped clean and bandage my hands, and Mike gave me back all the clothes I had given to the two guys earlier. Eric and Greg never knew that what I had given them was all I had, and when Mike found out what happened, he asked them to give back the clothing. They obliged, and Eric wrote me a note saying, "Daniel, I hope and wish that you get the most out of THE JOURNEY. May YAHWEH Bless You and Yours. Sincerely, Eric—Peace."

It had taken a lot of faith to give up my clothes, but in the end, that gesture left a lasting impact on both them and me; I was blessed tremendously through it all. Mike even gave me a dark blue down North Face jacket, saying I should take it because the desert gets cold at night. While my hands healed, it wasn't all rest and relaxation. The day after I arrived, we went to a church member's property to help herd cattle, but I did more watching than helping. Later in the week, we drove up one of the mountains overlooking Albuquerque, where we took some photos and had a great time. As my hands healed, I had the chance to practice playing Liana's guitar, which I really enjoyed.

That weekend brought a wonderful surprise: The Albuquerque Balloon Fiesta. I had no idea what it was until Liana mentioned it over dinner on Friday night.

"You've never heard of it?" she said in excitement. "Oh, you're in for a treat. We're going tomorrow morning, and you're coming with us."

The next morning, well before sunrise, we piled into their SUV. Everyone was bundled up in jackets while holding travel mugs of hot coffee. The girls were half asleep in the back seat, but the energy picked up the closer we got to the city.

As we broke through the mountain pass, the horizon lit up with hundreds of hot air balloons scattered across the sky. Towering shapes drifted gracefully above us, their colors glowing in the morning light. Reds, blues, and yellows in every pattern imaginable filled the view, turning the sky into a moving masterpiece.

"Look at that one," Torah shouted, pointing to a balloon shaped like a giant cow.

"That's so wild," I said, laughing.

Mike finally made it to the spot where he liked to watch the balloons. We stood together watching hundreds of balloons rise silently into the crisp morning air, and I felt a quiet joy in that moment. I was surrounded by strangers who felt like family, sharing something magical I never would have found on my own.

During my extended stay, Mike drove me about fifty miles north to Santa Fe, a place I had long wanted to visit ever since a childhood song first planted it on my mental map. We had a great time exploring the historic streets together and eating at a local restaurant. None of this would have happened if I hadn't fallen off my longboard. What seemed like a setback became the catalyst for some of the most meaningful experiences of my journey. I not only was able to deepen my bond with Mike and his family, but I was also able to explore new places and even speak to the youth group and lead worship with the guitar at their church. It's funny how something that feels like a misstep can lead to unexpected blessings.

When the time came for me to continue my journey, Mike, Liana, Torah, and Rhema drove me back to the spot where Mike had picked me up after my fall. We took some pictures together, shared some laughs, and said our goodbyes. Rhema didn't want me to leave and started crying again, just like the first time. It was tough to go, but I was grateful for the time together.

It took me nine more days to reach the New Mexico–Arizona border. Nearly my entire journey through New Mexico had been along the shoulder of I-40. Through the rest of the state, I was fortunate to stay with four more generous hosts, for whom I'm incredibly grateful. They were all friends and relatives of people I met along the way or those following me on social media. It was great because I didn't have to sleep under the New Mexico sky again and risk any tarantulas crawling on me.

As I ventured west of Albuquerque, the landscape shifted dramatically. Towering mesas and rugged buttes carved out of red sandstone rose along the horizon like ancient monuments. The flat desert floor gave way to massive cliff walls, streaked with layers of rust-colored rock that glowed under the sun. In the distance, flat-topped plateaus stood like natural fortresses, and the road cut through vast, open valleys where the sky felt impossibly big.

Near Gallup, I followed the highway as it curved beneath sheer canyon walls, some with caves and weather-worn alcoves etched into their faces. The terrain was dry and wild, dotted with low brush, distant trains, and the occasional weathered outpost beneath rock. It felt like every one of those rocks could have told me some wild west stories. This stretch of New Mexico didn't just take my breath away; it humbled me.

My first big fall scraped and bloodied my hands, but it also led to deeper connections, moments of unexpected kindness, and blessings I hadn't anticipated. The physical scars were a constant reminder of the challenges I faced, but they also told a story of resilience and growth. I used to imagine that challenges slowed the journey, but now I believe they enrich the experience. Each setback taught me something valuable, deepening my appreciation for every step of the road ahead. New Mexico had left its mark on me, both on my hands and in my heart.

As I came closer to reaching Arizona, I realized that every moment of pain had a purpose. This journey wasn't just about reaching the end of the road, but it was about embracing everything it had to offer, no matter how difficult or surprising. Scarred, tired, and sore, I was more determined than ever to keep going.

CHAPTER 12.

THE DAY AFTER MY TWENTY-FIFTH BIRTHDAY

OCTOBER 21 — OCTOBER 27, 2019

LUPTON, ARIZONA, TO HUNTINGTON BEACH, CALIFORNIA

I used to imagine that the finish line was the greatest prize,
but now I believe that the true reward is found in the journey.

Taking pictures at the "Welcome to Arizona" sign in Lupton, Arizona, reignited the fire within me and gave me a renewed sense of motivation to finish this journey. It was Monday, October 21, and my plan was to continue down I-40 for 358 miles through Flagstaff and all the way to California. With no places lined up to stay, I figured I'd sleep under bridges on my air mattress, bundled up in all my clothes to stay warm if necessary. At roughly 8 miles an hour and 10 hours a day, I figured I could make it in about a week.

As I made my way through Arizona, I received that first exciting phone call from Keith and Elizabeth sharing the news of her pregnancy. She told me she was twelve weeks along, her voice full of joy. Before we hung up, they offered to bless me with a hotel room for the night in Holbrook, and it turned out to be exactly what I needed. I continued cruising along the interstate passing through Chambers, Arizona. I saw a "No Pedestrians Allowed" sign but decided it didn't apply to me since I wasn't technically walking, which felt like a convenient loophole. Not long after, I spotted another traveler up ahead, casually walking the same way as if the sign were merely a suggestion. When I caught up, I introduced myself, and we started talking. His name was Ken, and he'd been hitchhiking across the U.S.

"Where'd you come from?" I asked.

"Started out in Montana a couple months ago," he said. "Just making my way around the country. Wherever the rides or trains take me."

While we were talking, a guy in a small pickup truck pulled over and offered us a ride. There wasn't enough room inside for both Ken and me, but the driver invited me to hop into the bed of the truck. I wanted to continue hanging with Ken, so I agreed and jumped in the back. The truck sped down the interstate, and I couldn't help but appreciate the chance to cover some extra ground. The driver dropped me off in Holbrook, Arizona, because that was where my hotel was, but Ken kept riding with him. I was a bit sad because I wanted to talk to Ken a little more. He seemed like a nice, authentic person, but now he was gone.

After sixty-seven miles, I was rewarded with a hot shower, a swimming pool, and a hot tub, which felt like a small slice of heaven. That night, I set a wake-up call for 5 a.m. because I wanted to reach Flagstaff, 90 miles away. Before sunset, a friend from social media offered to cover another hotel room, and that unexpected kindness felt like a hug from the Internet. Finally, after all those miles, I rolled into Flagstaff and, to my surprise, bumped into Ken again. I was genuinely glad to see him and asked where he planned to stay for the night.

"Wherever I can find a spot," he said.

Wanting to help, I messaged my social media friend and asked if they could book a room with two beds so Ken could join me. They agreed, and when I offered Ken the room, he didn't hesitate to say yes.

That night, we both enjoyed the comforts of a warm shower and relaxed in the hot tub. We swam around in the pool, shared some laughs, and just enjoyed each other's company. Back in the room, I offered Ken my favorite shirt, a light-blue Patagonia T-shirt. Ken only had the shirt on his back, and we needed to wash our clothes, so I offered him to wear mine. After doing our laundry, he fell asleep on the bed holding a cup of tea he had grabbed from the hotel lobby.

The next morning, I slept in and didn't get up before sunrise. The weather had started to cool down now that I was in Flagstaff. My goal was to reach Seligman next, about seventy-five miles away. Ken was still wearing my shirt as we headed down to breakfast. There was an amazing spread of bacon, eggs, sausage, pancakes, toast, and more: it was a feast for us. After breakfast, we checked out early, and I hit the road again, but not before snapping a quick picture with Ken and saying our goodbyes. I told him to keep the shirt because I could see he needed it more than I did.

After a couple hours of longboarding, a guy in a Toyota 4Runner stopped and asked if I needed a ride. At this point, I was less rigid about accepting help, realizing that connecting with people was more important to me than riding every mile on my longboard.

"Hey, I'm Daniel," I said. "I'd love a ride."

"I'm Branden. Hop on in. I hope you don't mind dogs," he said, nodding toward the old German shepherd and white husky-looking dog in the back seat.

I climbed in, and we ended up going on a little adventure. Branden offered to take a scenic drive up Bill Williams Mountain, a local landmark named after a nineteenth-century scout, guide, and mountain man who once roamed the American West. The mountain rose over 9,000 feet and stood just outside of Williams, Arizona, roughly halfway between Flagstaff and Seligman. The winding road to the top offered sweeping views of pine-covered slopes and distant plateaus that stretched out toward the horizon.

As we drove, we talked about life, snapped photos of the landscape, and listened to the album *Keep Going* by Mike Posner. At one point, Matisyahu came on, and we both started singing along. That turned into us freestyle-rapping in his 4Runner, and eventually we even traded poetry we had written. There was something surprisingly refreshing about it all, two strangers connecting over music, words, and wide-open views.

I treated Branden to lunch in Ash Fork. Over burgers and fries, I told him about my journey and how Jesus had changed my life. He listened quietly, nodding in that slow, thoughtful way people do when they are taking something in. I hoped it wasn't falling on deaf ears. Maybe I planted a seed, and sometimes that is enough. After we parted, I longboarded another twenty-five miles toward Seligman. It had been a few hours, and dusk was setting in. As I rolled closer to town, a car pulled over. An older man with white hair leaned over his passenger, a Native American woman who watched with amused patience, and called out, "Hey buddy, do you need a lift?"

"That would be great," I said. "I'm Daniel."

"My name's Mitch, and this is Kaya."

I climbed into the back, where I noticed a pizza box. Mitch looked over his shoulder and said, "It's been sitting there for about an hour, but if you're hungry, it's yours." I ended up eating the entire thing on the drive to Bullhead City.

On the way, Mitch asked about my board and what I was doing.

"I'm longboarding across America," I told him.

"That's pretty wild. Seems like you're also hitchhiking part of the way."

"Well, I decided to accept rides recently, only if people offer, because my trip is more about connecting with others than being on my board."

"I can take you as far as Bullhead City. Do you have a place to stay?"

"Not yet. I'm just trusting that the Lord will provide."

"Well, I've got an RV in a trailer park. You can stay there with us tonight if you'd like."

When we arrived, there was his RV. It was an older Class A motorhome with faded maroon-and-white stripes stretching down its long, boxy frame. The front windshield was wide and slightly weathered, with curtains drawn tight behind the glass to block out the desert sun. I leaned my longboard casually against the side of it. There were folding chairs, a cooler, and the kind of laid-back clutter that says someone's been living free for a while. It wasn't glamorous, but it had character. Just like my new friend.

Mitch was laid-back and loved to smoke cigarettes, laugh, and chat. We spent the evening getting to know each other and swapping stories. Later that night, Mitch needed to pick up a car from a hotel in California, which was just over the border from Bullhead City. He asked if I would help him by driving it back for him. I was once again struck by how trusting people were of me. It was one of those moments where I felt a deep connection with people I had just met, and it kept fueling my faith in the kindness and trust of strangers. I told him I'd be happy to help him out, so around 8 p.m., we drove about an hour into California to pick up a Chevy sedan.

The following morning, Thursday, October 24, I slept in a bit and then Mitch drove me to the California border on I-40. He snapped a picture of me standing next to the "Welcome to California" sign, marking another huge milestone in my journey. With that sense of accomplishment pushing me forward, I was confident that each day would bring new experiences and connections. I had no clue where I would sleep that night, but I trusted that God would guide me to a safe place.

I cruised down I-40 until I hopped onto US Route 95 heading south and soon saw a sign that read NEXT SERVICE 49 MILES. I was in the Mojave Desert, heading for Vidal Junction, where Route 95 crossed Route 62. After about forty miles, I finally arrived at the gas station on the corner of this remote intersection; it felt like an oasis. There were a handful of buildings surrounded by endless sand and brush. Inside the gas station, I grabbed something to eat and drink and took it up to the cashier. "Is that a skateboard?" she asked.

"It's a longboard, which is basically the same thing," I said.

"Are you riding that through the desert? Where did you come from?"

"I've been longboarding across the U,S. I came from Miami, Florida. What's your name?"

"I'm Bonnie. That's so wild. You must have run into a lot of adventure on your way. You better be careful going through the desert. It's easy to underestimate the heat during the day and the cold at night," she warned. I handed her a twenty to pay for my food. "Don't worry about it; this is on the house." Her generosity meant a lot, especially in such a desolate place.

As I ate outside on a picnic table, I noticed a guy on a bicycle who looked like he'd been traveling for a long distance.

I started a conversation with him and found out that his name was Michael, and he had been cycling all the way from New York City. It was pretty amazing that two people from the opposite sides of the country would meet at this random desert intersection. Michael was setting up his gear behind the gas station to sleep for the night, exhausted from a day of cycling, but I was gearing up for something different. I knew I had to continue through the desert that night.

The next town was 97 miles (156 kilometers) away, and there was absolutely nothing in between, just mountains and sand. It was the longest distance I'd have to travel without being able to stop for water. If I slept at night and boarded during the day, I would quickly run out of water. I only had 2 700-milliliter Nalgene water bottles with me, so I filled them one last time before leaving the gas station. After saying goodbye to Bonnie and Michael, I headed out into the desert at 6:30 in the evening, just as the sun began to dip below the horizon. A few miles down the road, I passed a sign that read TWENTYNINE PALMS 93 MILES. I knew it was going to be a long night, but I was determined to push through and reach my destination.

The desert was pitch dark, and the temperature dropped to the low sixties. I was glad for the coat Pastor Mike had given me. I had no cell phone service, and every five miles or so, I'd pass an old blue emergency call box, but they weren't exactly reassuring. By the time I hit the forty-mile mark, I was beyond exhausted. I reached the only stop sign in this endless desert stretch, a quiet crossroads in the middle of nowhere. With fatigue setting in hard, I blew up my air mattress and lay down next to a green electrical box with a blue sign above it that read CALL BOX. It was across the street from the scenic pull-off. I wondered if any creatures might crawl on me during the night. Between thoughts of arachnids and the cold, I barely got any rest and was back on my feet by 4 a.m., just before sunrise on October 25.

Twentynine Palms was still 51 miles (82 kilometers) away. I took a right at that intersection to continue west on Route 62, also known as Twentynine Palms Highway. The road was utterly desolate. A car would pass by maybe every fifteen minutes. By 8:30 a.m., I was down to my last 100 milliliters of water, less than half a cup. With the rising sun came the warmth. The early morning temperature was now in the fifties, but the air was desert dry. I prayed for water, took a deep breath, and then drank the last bit of it, trusting that God would provide.

Just as I closed the cap on my empty bottle, I heard the rumble of a motorcycle approaching from behind. The rider coasted to a stop, turned off his engine, and took off his helmet. He looked at me and asked, "Hey, Bro, what are you doing out here?"

"I'm longboarding across the United States," I said without hesitation.

The guy raised an eyebrow and then asked, "Well, do you need any water?"

I couldn't believe how quickly my prayer was answered. He reached into his backpack, pulled out a water bottle, and poured the whole thing into mine. I was overwhelmed with gratitude.

"There you go, man," the guy said as he handed back my bottle.

"Thank you so much. I had just prayed that God would provide as I took my last sip, and then you showed up. I can't thank you enough."

"It's no problem. We gotta look out for each other on the road, especially in the desert. You take care now." Then the guy put his helmet back on, revved up his motorcycle, waved, and disappeared down the road, leaving me with a refilled water bottle and a heart full of gratitude.

As I pressed on, the heat increased. By noon, it was up about seventy-five degrees. A few hours later, I was once again running low on water when Michael caught up with me on his bicycle. He had spent the night behind the gas station back at Vidal Junction and managed to catch up to me around noon. He could go about twice as fast on his bicycle as I could on my longboard.

"Need some water?" he asked. I did and gratefully accepted. Once again, my bottle was refilled. We cruised down the road together for a while. Eventually, Michael pulled ahead, and we agreed to meet up in Twentynine Palms later.

At 1:30 p.m., on Friday, October 25, I crossed into the city limits of Twentynine Palms. I had longboarded 100 miles in 24 hours, a personal record that I still haven't surpassed. Exhausted but exhilarated, I met up with Michael at Rocky's New York Style Pizza. I was so hungry and thirsty, I downed a few glasses of water and devoured an entire large pizza by myself. It was one of the most satisfying meals of my life after such an intense stretch of the journey.

After lunch, Michael continued his journey, while I lingered at the restaurant to catch up on messages and social media updates. I called a few friends and family members. It was nice to rest and reconnect with them after such a physically demanding day. As the evening set in and the temperature dropped, I packed up and hit the road again, longboarding another fifteen miles to Joshua Tree.

When I arrived, I found a spot to sleep under one of the iconic trees. The night air was cold, and despite wrapping my legs with all the extra clothing I had in my backpack and the coat Mike gave me, I could still feel the chill. As I huddled up under the branches of the tree and the stars above, I found comfort in my memories of the people who had helped me along the way. At 6 a.m., I stood up just as the sky began to brighten. It was my birthday, and the first thing I did was call my mom. After that, I hit the road, longboarding 25 miles to I-10. Los Angeles was in my sights. My uncle Lance lived in Irvine and had offered to host me.

I longboarded on I-10 through Beaumont and Moreno Valley without a problem. But as I reached Riverside, the traffic thickened, and the energy shifted. Cars were weaving in and out, and the shoulder started to feel narrower by the mile. I must've looked out of place, because a young guy pulled over and leaned across the passenger seat.

"You alright, man? Need a lift?" he called out.

"Sure," I said, catching my breath. "Honestly, that'd be great."

"I'm Isaiah. Throw your board and backpack in the back seat and hop in."

I did just that, and then, as he pulled back onto the road, we started talking.

"So, where you headed?" he asked.

"Just one more day until I make it to the coast. I'm longboarding across the country, and after I reach the ocean, God willing, I'll continue to San Francisco."

His eyes widened. "No way. That's insane."

"And today's my birthday," I added.

He smiled. "Get outta here. Mine was yesterday."

We both laughed. There was this strange, instant connection between us, like we were supposed to cross paths. Before dropping me off near my uncle's exit, Isaiah reached into the center console and pulled out a small rock.

"I've had this for a while," he said. "Feels right that you should take it. Something to remember the moment."

I still have that rock. It is small, jagged, and unremarkable to anyone else, which is precisely why it is perfect. It turned out to be an unexpected twenty-fifth birthday present from a stranger who somehow understood what the trip was really about—not maps and miles but the people who handed me a story, offered a ride, or, in this case, a little piece of rock to carry with me.

My uncle Lance was thrilled to see me. He is actually my second cousin, but he is my parents' age, so I call him uncle. It was hard to believe I had made it all the way from Florida on a longboard, and arriving on my birthday made it feel like a proper milestone. Uncle Lance took me and his daughter Raine out to a nice restaurant. We spent the evening catching up, swapping stories, and enjoying a great meal. It was the perfect way to mark the miles I had covered and celebrate another year.

That night, I slept so well. The next morning was Sunday, October 27, 2019. My uncle pastored the First Presbyterian Church in Santa Ana and was getting ready to drive there for the morning service. Instead of riding with him, I decided to longboard to the church since it was on the way to the beach. My plan was to head to Huntington Beach and complete my coast-to-coast longboarding goal after the service. The church was only about 15 miles from the beach, about a 2-hour ride. I wanted to end up at Huntington Beach because Jonathan

Stoltzfus and Trevor Heinrich had finished their walk across America at that very beach. Plus, my mom grew up in a town named Huntington, but the one on Long Island, New York. It felt fitting to finish there and follow in my friends' footsteps, especially as I would be wearing Trevor's vest to the beach for the second time. It was a way to honor his memory and connect our journeys.

The day couldn't have been more perfect. The sun was shining bright, and the air was warm; it was a typical day for Southern California. I stopped at a fruit stand where a woman sliced up a colorful array of fresh fruit and sprinkled Tapatío spice on top. The sweet, tangy flavors exploded in my mouth, adding more joy to the moment.

As I followed a bike path beside a water canal that seemed to point straight for the ocean, the weight of it all settled in. My dream was almost complete. Suddenly, I remembered where it had begun—Wisconsin, on that 13-mile skate the day after my 19th birthday. I had not thought of that trip in years, and now, the day after my twenty-fifth, I was staring at the finish line of something I had once only dared to imagine. It had been exactly six years, to the very day. And both days were Sunday afternoons. A deep sense of awe washed over me. Somehow, without any planning or awareness, God had brought me full circle.

It felt as though I had made a promise to myself six years ago, and now I was fulfilling it. I called my friends Kim from Pennsylvania and Will from Mississippi, along with family members who had been cheering me on throughout the journey. I told them the moment was finally here: I was about to see the ocean. When the horizon opened up to reveal the vast stretch of water, I felt an indescribable wave of emotions.

The relief and joy of knowing how far I'd come washed over me like the tide. I hopped onto the bike path that ran along the beach and captured a video to memorialize that moment.

My uncle showed up to record a video of me jumping into the ocean. It was a momentous occasion. And as I gazed out at the vast ocean, I knew that the miles I had traveled, the connections I had made, and the challenges I had overcome were true gifts. I used to imagine that the finish line marked the victory, but now I believe the journey is the real reward. Every push of the longboard, every answered prayer, every unique encounter, and every moment of faith had led me here. The journey had already given me more than I ever could have imagined, changing me in ways I didn't fully understand yet.

While the road to the Golden Gate awaited, I stood on the edge of the ocean with a deep sense of gratitude for everything the journey had already taught me. Little did I know, just as I was nearing the finish line, everything would take an unexpected turn. The longboard that had carried me across the country, my source of transportation and companion, was about to be stolen. The road to San Francisco would not be as straightforward as I thought.

CHAPTER 13.

STOLEN LONGBOARD

OCTOBER 27 – NOVEMBER 20, 2019
HUNTINGTON BEACH TO MONTEREY, CALIFORNIA

I used to imagine that revenge was justice,
but now I believe that forgiveness is the strongest choice.

After celebrating the completion of my coast-to-coast longboarding journey at Huntington Beach, I knew the adventure wasn't quite over. I still had miles to go before reaching the Golden Gate Bridge, but first, there was something else I was excited about. A few days earlier, I had reached out to the company that made my board, Loaded Boards, to tell them about my journey. To my surprise, they invited me to visit their warehouse in Culver City, California; it was an opportunity I couldn't pass up.

When I arrived, I was greeted by one of their employees, Ethan, who gave me a tour. It felt surreal to be in the very space where the board I had ridden across the country had come from. After my tour, I met Don Tashman, the founder and CEO. He signed my longboard, marking a special moment in my journey.

They took me downstairs, where they assemble and package their boards, and let me ride one of their electric Boosted Boards around the block. It was exhilarating, and I couldn't help but think how nice it would've been to ride that across America. While I was out riding, they surprised me by upgrading my longboard. They gave me brand new trucks, wheels, and bearings. When I returned, my board look like new; they even gifted me a fresh pair of slide gloves. Everything together was probably worth $300, and I was incredibly grateful for their generosity.

While in Southern California, I reconnected with a few different friends and relatives who generously hosted me as

I made my way north. My aunt Kim, uncle David, and cousin Elizabeth, who lived in Thousand Oaks, took me in for a week. We spent some quality time together and did a lot of surfing. Over dinner one night, I mentioned my plan to longboard through Big Sur on Highway 1.

"You sure about that?" my uncle asked, raising an eyebrow. "Those cliffs are no joke. It's beautiful, but that stretch of Highway 1 can be brutal, even in a car."

"Yeah," my aunt added. "People don't realize how narrow and winding those roads are. Maybe there's a safer way."

Frankly, I had been weighing a few things. First, I had already completed my original goal of going coast to coast. Second, longboarding through Big Sur would add several extra days or weeks, and by that point, I was ready for the journey to be over. After doing a little research, I found a small flight from Santa Barbara to Monterey, and thanks to my sister's flight benefits, it wouldn't cost me a thing.

Once in Monterey, I met up with my friend Lauren. She hosted me for the night and then introduced me to a friend, who generously let me stay the following evening. It felt like the home stretch was beginning to unfold, one connection leading to another, carrying me closer to the finish.

It was a mild Wednesday, November 20, and I decided to longboard around Monterey, grab lunch, and then head to Starbucks to read a book. I had been reading *The Traveler's Gift* by Andy Andrews, so I settled into a comfy chair and got to reading. After about twenty minutes, I stood up to use the bathroom. A group of teenagers walked in right then, looking like they had just been let out of high school for the day.

I returned to my seat and continued reading for another twenty minutes or so. When I was ready to leave, I went to the door where I had left my board, but it was gone. Throughout my journey across America, I had always trusted that God was watching over me and my board, so I never felt the need to guard it. I believed God was protecting it.

But now, just 120 miles from the Golden Gate Bridge, my board had been stolen. One moment it was leaning up against the wall in Starbucks; the next moment it had vanished as if it had grown legs and a better plan. I immediately walked outside and scanned the street for any sign of it, but there was no one around. Back inside, the manager listened with the sympathy of someone who had seen the same, small tragedy a thousand times. "It will take a couple weeks to pull the video footage from corporate," she said. Theft, it turned out, was a hobby in that store.

When I told her that I had used it to longboard all the way from Miami, Florida, her eyebrows went up in genuine surprise and then dropped with regret, making me feel like all hope was lost. The shiny new trucks and wheels Loaded Boards had just fitted were gone too. I mentioned the hundreds of signatures from people I'd met across America, which probably did not make her feel any better since there was nothing she could do. I told her I was going outside to see if I could find it.

When I walked out the door, I recorded a video to document the situation. I wasn't planning to post it, but I wanted to keep a record of what had happened, and I'm glad I did. I said, "As of right now, my board has been stolen, but I trust that God has a purpose for this. Whatever that may be, I'm fine with it. I'm just praying that I get it back. I'm gonna walk around and look for it, but it might be gone forever." As I spoke those words, my heart sank. Then I continued, "It's just a thing, and things come and go, so it's alright because I know that God's in control." I turned off the video, took a deep breath and prayed, "God, please take me to the thief!"

Just then, I heard the distant clatter of skateboards behind me. I thought maybe I should go talk to them, but then I reminded myself, *Don't rely on your own logic to figure this out. Have faith that God will take you to the thief.* And so, I kept walking forward, about a quarter mile, until I reached the bay. And there, sitting on a bench by the water, were two teenage boys holding my longboard as if it were a rare artifact.

They didn't hear me sneaking up behind them because they were too busy looking at all the signatures, art, and Bible verses scribbled on the bottom. Especially the one that said, "Thou shalt not steal." I'm kidding, but honestly, my first instinct was to snatch my board back and administer a swift, educational whack.

Instead, God quietly reminded me to swallow the anger and offer kindness, so I did. But I wasn't going to announce my arrival. I was just going to sneak up on them and grab it so they wouldn't be able to get away. And just before I began my approach, I pulled out my phone and started recording, because nothing diffuses a dramatic retrieval like the sober business of filming it.

As I grabbed the board, the kid holding it looked startled and asked, "Is that yours, Bro?"

"Yeah," I responded.

"I found that at Starbucks. Shoot, I was looking for a phone number," he stammered, trying to convince me he was a responsible thief.

"I longboarded across America with this board."

"I figured," he replied, "it looks important."

"Yeah," I told him, "so I don't really know why you stole it, but I actually prayed that God would take me right to you. So, I walked right over here from Starbucks and found my board. I'm Daniel," I said, holding out my hand. I shook their hands and asked the two boys their names. After they told me, I let them know I wasn't mad because I used to be a thief myself. I explained how I used to steal clothes from stores and candy from Walgreens, but I didn't do that anymore because Jesus had changed my life.

I then asked if I could pray for them, and they both immediately said yes as they bowed their heads. I just prayed peace and blessings over them, and, after I finished, we took a selfie together. Then the one who had taken my board asked if I had social media and started following me on Instagram. The next day, he sent me a message saying he was glad I had found my board; I think it was his way of apologizing. He also mentioned that a couple of years back, someone had stolen his longboard.

It's interesting how hurt people hurt people. It's a cycle we can get caught in. When someone wrongs us, we feel justified in wronging others. But returning evil for evil doesn't heal anything; it only makes the world worse. Thankfully, Jesus has shown us another way. He taught that we can live in the kingdom of heaven by forgiving others when they wrong us and acting as if we haven't been wronged at all.

Sometimes we only think of the kingdom of heaven as the place we go when we die, but actually, Jesus said that the kingdom is within you (Luke 17:21). When you let Jesus sit on the throne of your heart, your actions begin to change. Initially, I wanted to grab my board, chase them off, and maybe even hit them out of frustration, but what good would that have done? That continues the evil cycle. Now that Jesus sits on the throne of my life, I choose the actions He desires of me. And it turns out that the godly response had a far greater impact than the one I initially wanted to act on.

I believe forgiveness can heal the world, so I forgave those kids. I often wonder what the world would be like if one day everyone decided to forgive and act as if they had never been wronged. Imagine what your family would be like if everyone chose to forgive each other. No more grudges, no silent treatment, no digging up old wounds. Just real, honest reconciliation. Now picture that kind of forgiveness spreading to your neighborhood, your community, your city. What if it reached your nation? Imagine the impact if world leaders, presidents, prime ministers, and even dictators chose to release every offense and lead with mercy instead of revenge. The ripple effect would be unstoppable, transforming relationships, cultures, and the entire world.

Jesus is the best example in the history of the world of loving your neighbor. He never did one thing wrong; He always did what was right, yet He was wronged to the point of being unjustly killed. Imagine that! Never doing one thing wrong, not one thing, and then going to trial and being condemned to death. Most of us would feel justified in getting back at the liars and evil people who would do such a thing. But not Jesus. As He was hanging on a cross between two criminals, He looked up and said, "Father, forgive them, for they know not what they do" (Luke 23:34).

That level of forgiveness is beyond what most of us can comprehend. Yet in that moment, Jesus set the ultimate example. He could have retaliated. He could have called down a legion of angels to stop the injustice, but instead, He chose to extend grace to those blinded by their own actions. No one can forgive like this on their own. No one can do this apart from the grace of God. He calls us to repent of our sins and let go of our bitterness and, in doing so, participate in something far greater, the healing of our hearts and, ultimately, healing for the world.

After saying farewell to the boys, I rode back to Starbucks. When I got inside, I lifted up my board to show the manager and said, "I found it!" She was floored. I told her that I prayed that God would take me to the thief, and He did!

"No way!" she exclaimed with wide eyes.

Then I responded, "Yahweh!" and pointed my finger up toward the skies.

I wish you could have seen her face. She was smiling so big, she could've eaten a banana sideways. With all the thefts that had happened at that Starbucks, she just couldn't believe I had gotten it back. With a huge smile, she said, "I'm gonna make you a drink. Anything you want, it's on the house." I ordered a latte, and when she handed it to me, she'd written "Happy Trails" on the cup. I asked her name, and she told me it was Elisabeth. I was honored to meet her. We chatted for a bit, and she even started following my journey on Instagram too.

Several years later, I received a message from Elisabeth:

"Honestly, after we met, I couldn't stop thinking about your journey, confidence, and overall enthusiasm for people, life, and adventure! When you came back and said, 'The Lord sent you in the right direction and you found your board,' I just knew He wanted me to meet you that day. I'd been having a rough few days, and you turned it around by reminding me that the Lord works in mysterious ways. TRUST. I'm so happy for you in this new adventure in your life."

Her message reminded me how often we don't realize the impact we have on those watching us. People are always watching, especially in crucial moments, and our actions can leave a lasting impression. I used to imagine that revenge was justice, but now I believe that forgiveness is the stronger choice. That day, forgiveness didn't just restore my longboard. I believe it created a ripple effect I never could have anticipated.

As I sat there sipping my latte, reflecting on the craziness of the past few hours, it hit me how intertwined everything had been. How each step of this journey was guided, not just for me but for others too. It was humbling to realize that even in the midst of what felt like a setback, there was a chance to show grace, share faith, and build connections that stretched beyond the moment. This journey wasn't just about skating from Miami to San Francisco: it was about trusting God, connecting with people, and sharing the lessons along the way. It was about understanding that every serendipitous encounter, act of generosity, and even every loss was opportunity for something deeper.

With my board back under my feet, I felt relieved and ready to push through the final 120 miles. I knew the finish line was within reach, but somehow, after all that had happened, I sensed there was still more to this journey than just getting to the Golden Gate Bridge.

CHAPTER 14.

THE FINISH LINE

NOVEMBER 20 – DECEMBER 7, 2019

MONTEREY TO SAN FRANCISCO, CALIFORNIA

I used to imagine that great adventures were for the fearless, but now I believe they're for anyone willing to take the first step of faith.

The end was in sight. After thousands of miles, countless experiences, and many wonderful encounters etched in my memory, I found myself within a hundred miles of my final destination, the Golden Gate Bridge. But before reaching the iconic symbol of my coast-to-coast journey, I had a few more stops to make, and each one left its own mark on this final stretch.

Leaving Monterey, I set my sights on Santa Cruz, which was fifty-three miles away. Gliding along the coast with the ocean waves on my left side, this serene stretch was pure bliss. The weather was perfect, the bike paths were plentiful, and all the pavement was smooth. I did my best to savor those last moments, but I was ready for the trip to come to an end.

I had longboarded through California for many miles when I eventually reached Santa Cruz on November 21, and the vibrant surf town welcomed me with its laid-back energy. The familiar sound of my longboard wheels rolling over pavement, paired with the sea breeze, and the mix of colorful beach cottages and weathered Victorian houses, made it clear that I had arrived somewhere special. I wanted to stay and explore more, but I still had 33 more miles to go, and they were uphill, over 2,300 feet of climbing followed by a steep 2,000-foot descent into San Jose, where my great Aunt Marilyn and Uncle Clare lived and were expecting me to be there by the end of the day.

I was exhausted. Every part of me wanted to skate over the mountain, but I had nothing left in the tank, and the sun had already set. It was dark, and I was behind schedule. I knew I didn't have it in me to cross this mountain after a full day of longboarding. I also didn't want to risk crossing the mountains in the dark or spend the night sleeping outside. So, after much hesitation, I gave in and booked a ride over the mountain.

It wasn't an easy decision, but I felt like it was the best one in the moment. When I arrived, their warm smiles and open arms told me it was the right one. Their cozy home offered a much-needed pause. It turned out to be a place to rest, reflect, and enjoy a slower pace, if only for a little while. One of the highlights of my time there was listening to Uncle Clare play the piano. The music filled the room, and for a moment, I just sat there, letting the classical melody wash over me. It felt like a gift to pause and appreciate the beauty of something so simple, yet so powerful.

The next day, they gave me a tour of the area, taking me through parts of Silicon Valley I had only ever heard about, driving by big tech campuses, historical spots, and beautiful neighborhoods with stories behind them. Later, we met some of their friends for lunch at the Old Spaghetti Factory. I was the youngest person at the table by far, but that didn't seem to matter.

At one point, a lady looked over at me and asked, "So, you really skated across the whole country?"

"Yep," I said, twirling spaghetti on my fork. "One push at a time."

She smiled and said, "That's incredible. The only thing I've crossed lately is a parking lot to get here."

Everyone laughed, and the conversation flowed from there. We shared stories and jokes and ate plates of pasta like old friends. It was one of those rare moments where age didn't matter: it was just about good food, good company, and enjoying the present.

In the afternoon, Aunt Marilyn took me to visit the famous Winchester Mansion in San Jose. The house started out as an 8-room farmhouse when Sarah Winchester bought it in 1896 after her husband, an heir to the Winchester Arms fortune, died of tuberculosis. For the next 38 years, she kept adding on to the house until it became a 24,000-square-foot giant with 160 rooms, 47 stairways and fireplaces, 27 chimneys, 13 bathrooms, and 6 kitchens. It was a fascinating place. Walking through it felt surreal, full of strange twists and turns, stairways that went nowhere, and rooms that seemed misplaced. In a way, it reminded me of my own journey, with moments that felt confusing at the time but often revealed something meaningful once I got through them.

After spending a couple of days with my aunt and uncle, it was time to keep moving. On November 23, I longboarded 25 miles north to Fremont, where my friends, the Dunfords, lived. Scott, my former college professor and vice president of Northland International University, and his family welcomed me into their home with open arms, and I felt the same sense of hospitality that had carried me across the country. The next morning, an old college friend, Sara, came by the house, and we all had a great time catching up. It was nice to be able to just pick up where we left off and catch up on each other's lives. I also met the Blaha family, friends of the Dunfords, who generously hosted me. My first night at their house, Ricky looked at me and jokingly said, "You're not just passing through; we're putting you to work."

I laughed. "As long as I can sleep inside, I'm down."

He paid me to do a small drywall repair in the dining room of their house, and I spent the afternoon measuring, cutting, and fixing up the wall. When I finished, Ricky handed me some cash and said, "This is for the road. You've earned it." It was a kind gesture that helped fund the last leg of my trip, and I was grateful, not only for their generosity but for the way they welcomed me like family.

On Thursday, December 5, I left Fremont and skated across the Dumbarton Bridge, gliding past the headquarters of Facebook and Instagram. It was surreal to have gone through Silicon Valley with nothing but a simple board, my legs, and a stubborn determination that no amount of innovation could buy. That afternoon, I rolled into South San Francisco and found Luke Valenzuela and his family waiting with open arms. We spent the evening swapping stories, laughing about everything, and enjoying a truly delicious home-cooked meal.

The following day, I spent time with Luke, and that evening, we went to a school Christmas play his nieces and nephews were in. I sat in a big row with the whole Valenzuela family there in the school's auditorium. Though it was a small production, watching the kids act out each scene stirred up childhood memories of performing in plays myself and celebrating holidays surrounded by family and friends.

As I sat there in the dimly lit auditorium, everything seemed to slow down. The laughter of the audience, the proud smiles on parents' faces, and the simple joy of the children on stage all settled around me. For a moment, I wasn't just watching a play; I was taking in the picture of a family knit closely together. After so many months on the road, meeting strangers who became friends but always moving on, I felt a longing rise in me to soon stop wandering, build a family of my own, and sit in a crowd like this watching my children grow and take the stage. When the night was over and everyone was gone, I laid down on the living room sofa and fell asleep to thoughts about a beautiful future, but first, I had to finish this trip.

The next morning, it was time. I had one final push ahead of me—longboarding from Luke's house to the Golden Gate Bridge. This was it. The moment I had been working toward for six long years. My heart was full of anticipation, gratitude, and a familiar sense of peace. I was only eight miles from the Golden Gate Bridge, and I had arranged for Luke to meet me there and capture the moment with some photos, then we would return to his house. Everyone wished me a safe trip to the bridge, and then I set off, longboarding north on Mission Street toward the bay. The city of San Francisco unfolded around me with scenery I'd only ever seen in movies like *The Princess Diaries* and *The Pursuit of Happyness*.

As I navigated the steep hills, the challenge reminded me of the ups and downs of the trip itself. I stopped at the bottom of a hill, glanced down, and spotted a two-dollar bill lying on the ground. It felt like a sign, a small token of favor on this final leg of my long adventure. I picked it up and continued longboarding down streets like O'Shaughnessy Boulevard and Nancy Pelosi Drive, knowing the bridge had to be close.

As I rounded a curve where Washington Boulevard meets Lincoln Boulevard, I pulled out my phone and recorded as the massive red towers came into view. There it was—the Golden Gate Bridge standing tall against the skyline. Seeing it in real life for the first time was overwhelming. "I made it to the Golden Gate Bridge!" I said to the camera. "All the way from Miami

Beach, Florida! Woo hoo! Let's go! There she is, boys!" I was ecstatic, overflowing with joy at having completed the journey.

Reaching the bridge wasn't enough. I had to longboard across it. I shot another video from the bridge, encouraging others to pursue their dreams and never give up. I also pointed out the unbelievable fact that it hadn't rained on me during the entire trip. Not once. I crossed to the far side of the bridge, took a selfie, and realized that this was it. The end was really here. Now, all I had to do was meet Luke.

I texted him and then crossed back to the south side of the bridge, where we had arranged to meet. When I saw him, he yelled out, "Congratulations!" We high-fived, then hugged and then he snapped several photos of me with the bridge in the background. The last picture he took was at 11:10 a.m., and the next minute, the skies opened up, and it started to pour rain. It was as if the clouds had waited until my trip was officially done.

We stopped taking pictures and headed for cover at the welcome center next to the bridge, trying to stay dry. As we stood there, a rainbow appeared over the bridge, perfectly framing the end of my journey. I pulled out my phone one last time to capture the moment, knowing I'd never forget it. "Oh my God!" I said. He had done it again. He made the most beautiful ending for me, reminding me of His faithfulness all along the way.

As I stood there under the rainbow, reflecting on my journey, I couldn't help but think of all the lessons I'd learned along the way. This adventure wasn't just about crossing the country on a longboard: it was about new relationships, real growth, deep faith, and discovering how to navigate life itself.

From the early days of battling through long stretches of road, I learned endurance: the ability to push through when things get hard. I discovered that true growth happens outside of your comfort zone, where you're stretched and forced to rely on a strength greater than your own. The road taught me that perseverance paired with faith can lead you to places you never thought you'd reach. It also taught me forgiveness.

And perhaps the most important lesson I learned is that God provides in every situation. It wasn't always in the ways I expected, but the provision was always there. When you have faith and trust that you're not going through life alone, your confidence is strengthened. An old Chinese proverb says that the journey of a thousand miles begins with a single step. In my case, the journey of three thousand miles began with a single push.

I used to imagine that dreams were meant for the fearless, but now I believe they're for anyone willing to take the first step in faith. If you have a dream, go for it. It may not feel like much at first, but every journey, no matter how daunting, is built one step at a time.

This journey wasn't just about faith and endurance. It was also about love. I met so many people from all walks of life, and I saw firsthand how much love can change someone's day, or even their life. Whether it was sharing a meal, offering a prayer, or simply lending a listening ear, brotherly love was at the center of every meaningful connection I made. And if there's one thing I've learned, it's that love is the force that keeps us all moving forward, no matter how different our paths may seem.

Here are the final words I want to leave you with. I wrote them down to remind myself what to do when times get hard. I call it the *Love and Longboard Manifesto*:

When an impossible dream is staring you in the face, never give up.

Keep moving forward when the road feels uncertain, for God is always with you and will provide for your needs.

Remember that yesterday is history, tomorrow's a mystery, and today is God's gift—that's why we call it the present.

Forgive quickly, for forgiveness gives your heart the freedom to keep going.

Treasure the people you meet along the way, for every encounter has it's purpose.

Embrace the journey, for within it lies the true reward.

Surrender each day to the commands of Christ and walk in His peace.

Above all, love deeply as you travel through life, whether you are walking, running, biking, or, like me, skateboarding across the country.

The road will not always be easy, but keep going.

Keep dreaming.

Keep loving.

And if you feel like it, longboard along the way.

A NOTE FROM THE AUTHOR

Thank you for reading this book. I continue to be encouraged, inspired, and challenged by these stories myself whenever I read them. I hope they did the same for you.

I'd be honored if you'd consider leaving a review wherever you purchased it. Every review helps this book reach more people.

Feel free to share the book or pass it along to a friend.

Interested in ordering 10 or more copies for your group, school or organization? Email hello@loveandlongboard.com for special bulk pricing.

Wishing you all the best as you continue your own journey.

Much love,
Daniel Herman Jr.

EPILOGUE

Happy endings are just the start of beautiful beginnings.

I completed my journey at the Golden Gate Bridge on December 7, 2019. Not long after, I accepted a job in Washington State building tiny homes in 2020, which became a new adventure of its own. That summer, I rode my Harley Davidson motorcycle around the country and revisited most of the people who I had met during my longboard journey. Eventually, I moved to South Carolina, where I reestablished my love for carpentry and started my own company.

In 2021, I met a beautiful girl named Stephanie who lived in Europe. What began as a conversation through social media turned into love, marriage, and two unforgettable years together in northeast Italy. Then we traveled the world together across four continents and twenty countries. We grew through incredible experiences that changed us both. When Stephanie's United States spouse visa was approved, we moved to South Carolina, restarted my carpentry company, and began building a life together. It wasn't long before we had our first baby girl named Rose Isla.

We live in a town called Campobello, which means "beautiful field," where we can watch the sun set behind the Blue Ridge mountains on the horizon. I want to leave my mark on the world and do my best to make it a better place. I believe this book is only the beginning of another journey, one where I hope to inspire others in faith, forgiveness, and love.

ACKNOWLEDGEMENTS

It takes a big cast to support a journey like this one. Writing a book is never a solo act, and neither is longboarding across America. This story is stitched together by a festival of friends, family, strangers who became companions, and the countless people whose kindness shaped the road beneath my wheels. Whether your name is written here or simply etched in my memory, know that your encouragement, prayers, meals, beds, and laughter carried me further than my legs alone ever could.

First and foremost, I owe a deep thanks to my sister Audrey, who first introduced me to longboarding. She may not know it, but her influence set me rolling on the path that became this book. To Tim Pacholski for opening my eyes to see the love God has for me and others. And to Kim Metzler, my greatest supporter and biggest fan, whose encouragement stretched back before this trip even began. You believed in me when the dream still felt impossible, and I will always be grateful.

There are others whose fingerprints are all over these pages. Nate and Krista Peavy, who extended such great hospitality and are like family to me, reminding me always that the love and forgiveness of God is unending. Richard Durousseau, who bought me breakfast and stayed in touch for years afterward. Jerrod Arredando, for friendship, prayer, and showing up at just the right times. Wayne Wallace, Kelly Wood, Becky Slayton, Betty and Larry Goff, Alice and Emma McKinney, Elizabeth Palmatier, John Garza, and especially Keith and Elizabeth Fry with Copper, you each played a role that turned hard miles into holy moments. Denise Hudson and Bobby, thank you for welcoming me into your home and going the extra mile to drive me back and forth so I could pick up the journey right where I left off.

Justin and Christy Hollingshead, thank you for opening your home and for the friendship that has continued through the years. Pastor Mike and Liana, along with Rhema and Torah, thank you for opening your home in New Mexico and refreshing my spirit while my hands healed. Jonathan Stoltzfus, for connecting me to people along the way and offering steady encouragement over the phone, and Trevor Heinrich, a brother in faith who gave me inspiration when I needed it most, may you rest in peace. Tristan Poss, my lifelong best friend since I was four, and his dearly missed dad, Doug, who had been more like a father to me than a friend; you both have been with me from the beginning, and I could not imagine this journey without your support. Reece, Danielle, and the Sarkela family, thank you not only for your friendships but also for the motorcycle y'all gave me. And to Debbie and her husband Fratt Aho, who has gone to be with Jesus but faithfully called me on the phone along the way; you both were a great encouragement during my journey.

My cousin Justin Matthews, thank you for stepping in and paying off my debt so that I could start this trip with a clean slate. Your generosity gave me the freedom to take the first push.

Jenny and Jeff Stone deserve special thanks for doing far more than opening their home. Jenny called so many news outlets I lost track, and those interviews changed the entire trajectory of my journey. Because of that publicity, more doors opened, more people followed along, and more kindness poured in than I ever could have imagined.

To the many who gave me food, water, shelter, or just met me along the way, Robert Wolk, Stacie Brandt, Kristin and the Davis family, Evan Talor, Terry, Keirnan, Reid and Victoria Sullivan, Stefanie and Claire Goyak, Chad and Dawn Massey, Chris Crouch, Cookie and Tresta, Shannon and Cassie Mhoon, Daris and the Adams family, Gil and Maggie Rennels, Paula at Coats Groceries, Pastor Seth Moore, Liz Tipps, Stephanie Phillips, Branden Larson, Isaiah Estanislao, Uncle Lance, Aunt Sophia and Raine, Uncle David, Aunt Kim and Elizabeth Herman, Uncle Clare and Aunt Marilyn, Scott, Tara and the Dunford family, Ricky, Karlyn and the Blaha family, Luke Valenzuela and his family and dozens more people, you reminded me that hospitality is one of the greatest gifts we can offer each other. To those I met in Coleman, Brownwood, Lampasas, Snyder, Muleshoe, Lubbock, Abilene, and Early, including Mayor Mike McMahan and the town of Goldthwaite, I am grateful. Thanks to the many business owners who cheered me on; your communities left a mark on me. To Captain Will Ladnier and his daughters Juliana and Aubrey, for teaching me the ways of life on the Gulf, and for showing me how to have fun and make the most of every situation. To Bonnie and Michael in the California desert, Lauren in Monterey, you each gave me warmth and belonging when I was far from home.

I am grateful as well to the voices who helped shape this book after the road was done. Geoffrey Stone, Blair Parke and Brooks Becker for editing and guiding my words, and Judy Durham for being the first to read them. Marko M. for designing a cover that captured the spirit of this journey. And to Jennifer Vest, thank you for giving me the very title of this book back in 2015, when the dream was still only a thought.

And finally, to my family. To my parents, Dan and Jeanne Anne Herman, for your love and support since birth. I love you both. To my sister Carol for her love and support, and the rest of my siblings: Audrey, Stephen, Nathan, Autumn, and Sophia. I love you all. To my wife, Stephanie, who has stood beside me on five continents as I wrote this book with patience and love, and to our daughter, Rose, who will one day read these words and know that her daddy once chased a dream across the country, you two are my greatest gifts. And above all, to my Lord and Savior Jesus Christ, whose faithfulness carried me through the deserts, over the mountains, and every mile in between. This book, this journey, and this life are for You.

ABOUT THE AUTHOR

Daniel Herman Jr. is an author, speaker, and craftsman whose life has been shaped by faith, adventure, and creativity. At 19, he imagined longboarding across America, and 6 years later, he made that dream a reality by skating 3,200 miles from Miami to San Francisco. That journey became the heart of his first book, *Love and Longboard*, a story about love, faith, and forgiveness, and how God meets us in the middle of impossible dreams and unexpected challenges.

When he is not writing, Daniel is often creating with his hands and finding joy in building and making. He and his wife, Stephanie, enjoy traveling, cooking, and raising their daughter, Rose. Whether sharing stories, working on projects, or encouraging others to take their own step of faith, Daniel seeks to inspire people to live with courage, chase the impossible, and hold fast to faith, forgiveness and love.

CONNECT WITH DANIEL

One of the things I have learned from this journey is how much people matter. The miles were important, but what truly shaped me were the people I met along the way, even if just for a moment. Their kindness, encouragement, and availability left a mark on my life that went far beyond the road. I hope this book does the same for you.

If something in these pages spoke to you, I would love to hear from you. You can reach me at hello@loveandlongboard.com or visit my website at www.loveandlongboard.com. I am also on Facebook at Daniel Ray Herman Jr., and you can find me on Instagram, TikTok, and X @Everyday.Dan. Let's stay connected and keep encouraging each other to take bold steps of faith.

www.ingramcontent.com/pod-product-compliance
Ingram Content Group UK Ltd.
Pitfield, Milton Keynes, MK11 3LW, UK
UKHW041631190726
13854UKWH00006B/2420